ining, stimul

occasionally

of view that

ion of, or in

ly originate

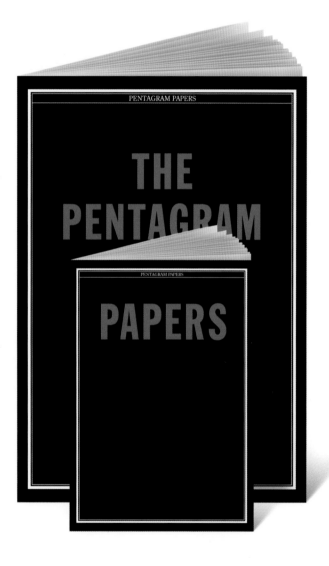

THE PENTAGRAM PAPERS

A collection of thirty-six papers
containing curious, entertaining,
stimulating, provocative,
and occasionally controversial
points of view that have
come to the attention of, or in
some cases are actually
originated by, the partners
of Pentagram Design

Created by

the Pentagram Partners

Edited by Delphine Hirasuna

Designed by Kit Hinrichs

 Thames & Hudson

CONTENTS

A partnership begun in 1972 by five designers in diverse disciplines, Pentagram has grown to twenty partners, who maintain independent practices while sharing resources and revenues.

A discussion started on a train ride in the mid-seventies led to the establishment of a quirky, eclectic, and memorable set of black books called the Pentagram Papers.

CONTENTS

PENTAGRAM PAPERS

1

9

PENTAGRAM PAPERS

7

PENTAGRAM PAPERS

2

PENTAGRAM PAPERS

The Pentagram Partnership

In the world of design, Pentagram has long had a special cachet. Not a partnership in the traditional sense, it is more a consortium of creative minds that have joined together for the opportunity to explore ideas outside the bounds of their specialties. Multidisciplinary, multinational, and multifaceted, Pentagram is not known for any single specific style—save for a concept-driven approach that spurns the decorative or trendy. Yet over the last three decades, perhaps no other design firm in the world has had such a sweeping and powerful impact on the visual presentation of business and culture as Pentagram. Its design influence is visible worldwide in corporate brands and communications, exhibitions and interiors, national magazines and catalogs, packaging and consumer products, interactive media and print publishing, architecture and signage, posters and postage stamps, to list just a few areas.

Now comprising twenty partners based in offices in London, Berlin, New York, San Francisco, and Austin, Pentagram operates on a model that impresses and confounds those in the business. It is, in essence, twenty "independent" practices that equally share profit and loss and management authority. Partners pursue their

own projects and manage their own teams. Although the global scope of businesses today and the overlapping nature of design disciplines have increased collaboration among Pentagram offices and partners, the consultancy fiercely values the dynamic tension created by partners with diverse views. This is a characteristic that has been part of Pentagram from the start.

Founded in London in 1972, Pentagram adopted its five-sided name when the design office of Theo Crosby, Alan Fletcher, and Colin Forbes joined forces with Kenneth Grange and Mervyn Kurlansky. Even then, the firm was multidisciplinary—Crosby an architect; Grange an industrial designer; and Fletcher, Forbes, and Kurlansky graphic designers but with decidedly different points of view. Each came to the partnership with a well-established reputation and a portfolio that included some of the most celebrated design of their time. Their reasons for joining together had little to do with an inability to thrive on their own.

All in their late thirties and forties when they formed Pentagram, the original partners had individually arrived

Kenneth Grange

Mervyn Kurlansky

Original Five: 1972
The partners named their firm Pentagram because it described their business structure and aspirations: "A star of five equal points, with alternating points connected by a continuous line; symbolic of alchemy."

at a juncture in their careers where the administrative and marketing demands of growing their business beyond a certain point left them with little freedom to do what they loved best, namely design. Their desire to pursue commissions that provided greater personal satisfaction and to move beyond their particular design discipline led them to see the advantages of sharing administrative burdens. At the same time, what each adamantly refused to give up was creative autonomy. From day one, Pentagram was structured to allow partners to run their own teams under the auspice of the consultancy, while pooling resources and collaborating when appropriate.

Robert Brunner

Michael Bierut

Lisa Strausfeld

Angus Hyland

John McConnell

Kit Hinrichs

Lorenzo Apicella

Daniel Weil

Fernando Gutiérrez

James Biber

Abbott Miller

David Hillman

Justus Oehler

John Rushworth

Michael Gericke

DJ Stout

Woody Pirtle

Paula Scher

Lowell Williams

A group photograph of the partners of Pentagram is a tradition at the semiannual partners' meetings, which are alternately held in Europe in the spring and in North America in the fall. This portrait was shot in 2004 in front of the historic Ver Sacrum building in Vienna, Austria.

That has remained the case to this day. Pentagram is a partnership of shared zeal for excellence and creative growth. Most of the partners have spent more than a decade running their own studio or heading the design function of a publication or company before joining the firm. Over the years, Pentagram has grown and shrunk and grown in number of partners, as first and second generation partners retire out and new designers join.

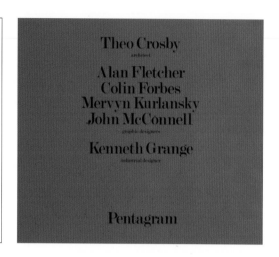

Theo Crosby
architect

Alan Fletcher
Colin Forbes
Mervyn Kurlansky
John McConnell
graphic designers

Kenneth Grange
industrial designer

Pentagram

For Pentagram, representing every design discipline has not been as essential as ensuring that each new partner is respected as among the best in the field.

An invitation to join Pentagram still has allure, even for the most successful designers—not just for the honor of being part of this illustrious firm, but for the same reasons that the founding partners chose to come together. They recognize that aggregating their abilities under the Pentagram umbrella will extend their individual credibility and allow them to pursue opportunities that may have seemed risky as independent practitioners.

Merging a group of creative and successful designers into a coequal partnership has its drawbacks, however. The nonhierarchical organization of Pentagram causes inevitable collisions among strong-willed individuals. But what makes the Pentagram model work are core beliefs held by all of the partners—namely, that content must drive design, that good design must be informed by the world around it, that creative excellence is as important as financial performance, that good design elevates quality of life for society as a whole, and that teaching the value of design is the responsibility of every practitioner.

Partners rally around these principles at their semi-annual meetings, which alternate between exotic locales in Europe and North America. These values underlie their esprit de corps and help them overlook their creative differences. If the partners are driven by a

Anniversary Memento
On the anniversary of the founding of the firm, Pentagram produces a commemorative gift for each partner. Mementos range from 21st year cup-and-saucer sets to limited edition art prints.

higher social purpose, they also hold each other to rigorous standards. At every meeting, they give formal presentations of their recent work. As cacophonous as these peer reviews can be, the feedback, sharing of personal experiences, and different perspectives stimulate fresh thinking and challenge everyone to consider solutions outside their comfort zone.

The culture of Pentagram encourages openness to diverse views and sees intellectual curiosity as necessary for creative innovation. These are qualities that the Pentagram partners demand from themselves and seek to foster in others. The Pentagram Papers series is dedicated to this purpose.

1972

London 1972

Theo Crosby
Alan Fletcher
Colin Forbes
Kenneth Grange
Mervyn Kurlansky

1973–1980

New York 1978

Colin Forbes ◄┄┄┄┄
Peter Harrison 1979

London

Theo Crosby
Alan Fletcher
Colin Forbes ┄┄┄┄┄
Kenneth Grange
Mervyn Kurlansky
John McConnell 1974
Ron Herron 1977–80*
David Hillman 1978

OPENED FIRST U.S. OFFICE

1981–1985

New York

Colin Forbes
Peter Harrison

London

Theo Crosby
Alan Fletcher
Kenneth Grange
Mervyn Kurlansky
John McConnell
David Hillman
David Pelham 1983–85*

1986–1990

New York

Colin Forbes
Peter Harrison
Etan Manasse 1987
Woody Pirtle 1988
Michael Bierut 1990

London

Theo Crosby
Alan Fletcher
Kenneth Grange
Mervyn Kurlansky
John McConnell
David Hillman
Howard Brown 1987†
John Rushworth 1989
Peter Saville 1990

San Francisco 1986

Kit Hinrichs
Linda Hinrichs
Neil Shakery

* Left Pentagram   ** Died   † Partner for less than one year

1991–1995

New York

Colin Forbes 1993*
Peter Harrison 1994*
Etan Manasse 1991**
Woody Pirtle
Michael Bierut
Paula Scher 1991
James Biber 1991
Michael Gericke 1993

Hong Kong 1994

David Hillman ◄

London

Theo Crosby 1994**
Alan Fletcher 1992*
Kenneth Grange
Mervyn Kurlansky 1993*
John McConnell
David Hillman ◄
John Rushworth
Peter Saville 1992*
David Pocknell 1992–94*
Daniel Weil 1992
Justus Oehler 1995

San Francisco

Kit Hinrichs
Linda Hinrichs 1991*
Neil Shakery 1994*
Lowell Williams 1992

Austin 1994

Lowell Williams ◄

1996–2000

New York

Woody Pirtle
Michael Bierut
Paula Scher
James Biber
Michael Gericke
Abbott Miller 1999

Hong Kong 1997

David Hillman

London

Kenneth Grange 1998*
John McConnell
David Hillman ◄
John Rushworth
Daniel Weil
Justus Oehler
Angus Hyland 1998
Lorenzo Apicella 1998
Fernando Gutiérrez 2000

San Francisco

Kit Hinrichs
Robert Brunner 1996

Austin

Lowell Williams
DJ Stout 2000

Los Angeles 2000

April Greiman

2001–2005

New York

Woody Pirtle 2005*
Michael Bierut
Paula Scher
James Biber
Michael Gericke
Abbott Miller
Lisa Strausfeld 2002

Berlin 2002

Justus Oehler ◄

London

John McConnell 2005*
David Hillman
John Rushworth
Daniel Weil
Justus Oehler ◄
Angus Hyland
Lorenzo Apicella
Fernando Gutiérrez
William Russell 2005

San Francisco

Kit Hinrichs
Robert Brunner

Austin

Lowell Williams
DJ Stout

Los Angeles 2001

April Greiman 2001*

2006

New York

Michael Bierut
Paula Scher
James Biber
Michael Gericke
Abbott Miller
Lisa Strausfeld

Berlin

Justus Oehler ◄

London

David Hillman
John Rushworth
Daniel Weil
Justus Oehler ◄
Angus Hyland
Lorenzo Apicella
Fernando Gutiérrez
William Russell
Domenic Lippa 2006
Harry Pearce 2006

San Francisco

Kit Hinrichs
Robert Brunner
Lorenzo Apicella 2006 ◄
DJ Stout 2006 ◄

Austin

Lowell Williams
DJ Stout

OPENED HONG KONG OFFICE, WORKED IN BOTH OFFICES

CLOSED HONG KONG OFFICE

OPENED BERLIN OFFICE, WORKS IN BOTH OFFICES

WORKS IN BOTH OFFICES

MOVED TO S.F. OFFICE

MOVED TO S.F. OFFICE

OPENED AUSTIN OFFICE

No. 1

The Beginning

While riding on a train between Amsterdam and the Hague in 1975, Pentagram partners John McConnell and Colin Forbes continued a discussion that had been ongoing among the partners—namely, what the firm's essential philosophy should be. They weighed partner Theo Crosby's conviction that Pentagram should be more theoretical and intellectual than other design firms, and they kept returning to a remark made by an admirer who told them that he considered Pentagram's multidisciplinary approach the nearest thing to the Bauhaus then in existence. Forbes and McConnell didn't take that flattering comparison seriously, but the notion of imparting more to the world than their commercial talent appealed to them. If anything bound the Pentagram partners together, it was their shared interest in teaching, passing on knowledge, and offering up thought-provoking ideas that extended beyond the self-promotional or clever.

These objectives guided the creation of the Pentagram Papers. The brainchild of McConnell, the concept as originally proposed was to publish a series of booklets on interesting topics that had been largely ignored elsewhere. Through design commissions, speaking tours, and international travels, the partners of Pentagram

often encountered people with fascinating obsessions and unique perspectives. Their colleagues often told them about "orphan" editorial projects that languished in drawers for lack of a publisher. The partners also collected or had friends who collected odd and commonplace things that really had to be studied as a set to appreciate the ingenuity and design styling that went into them. All of these sources offered possible material for Pentagram Papers.

"Pentagram Papers are not meant to be about selling what we do, but about communicating subjects that would be of interest to a wide range of people, from the managing director of a corporation to others in our field," explains McConnell. "It is saying, 'Isn't this interesting. It is something we came across and we thought you might find it interesting.'"

Given these parameters, partners are encouraged to nominate topics that they find intriguing. They do, complete with photographs and rough layouts, at the semiannual partners' meetings. The group votes to accept or reject the idea, and the partner who proposes the piece is responsible for seeing it through.

The diverse perspectives of the partners explain the idiosyncratic identity of the Pentagram Papers, a fact that the books readily admit by telling readers at the back of each book that these are "examples of curious, entertaining, stimulating, provocative and occasionally contro-

Pentagram Books
Pentagram produces a book about the firm every five years. In addition to showcasing the work of the partners, the books take an outward view of the business and reflect on the direction of design.

versial points of view that have come to the attention of, or in some cases are actually originated by, Pentagram."

Considering these loose guidelines, practically anything goes. What gives the Pentagram Papers series continuity is its consistent format and look. Over the past thirty years, virtually all of the volumes have been 5¾-by-8¼ inches (146-by-210 millimeters) in size, featuring a black cover with white ruled border and inside pages that are surprisingly understated, considering that they are published by one of the world's most renowned design firms. Until Americans joined the Pentagram partnership, most of the volumes were printed only in black-and-white. "The Americans couldn't live without color," McConnell says, ruing the day that this philistine change was allowed to happen.

Although some of the topics for Pentagram Papers originate from a partner's own personal interest, many come through colleagues and acquaintances. That was the case with the first Pentagram Paper, which presented the A-B-C portion of a dictionary of graphic clichés compiled by Philip Thompson and Peter Davenport.

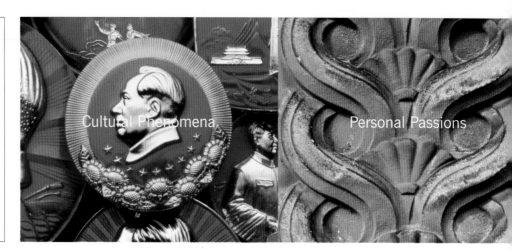

At the time, Thompson and Davenport lamented to McConnell that they couldn't find a publisher, which prompted McConnell to suggest that Pentagram print an excerpt. The exposure drew the attention of a publishing house, which subsequently published the entire book.

Often, however, topics that are not significant enough or large enough to be published as a full-length book prove ideal for a Pentagram Paper, which typically runs twenty-four to fifty-two pages. Partners hear of topics while chatting with friends or through serendipitous introductions to experts on esoteric subjects. Whenever possible, Pentagram tries to get someone with first-hand knowledge of the subject to contribute the text.

Pentagram Papers have a very select and limited distribution and very devoted following. The press run for early volumes was about two thousand copies, with runs of between four and six thousand copies for more recent editions. Recipients tend to treasure their copies and display their set of the thin black booklets prominently on their bookshelves. Over the years, the scarcity of copies has made them highly collectible.

Collections

Retrospection

Eclectic Content
What has made the Pentagram Papers so unique is their lack of predictability. A Paper on architecture may be followed by one on souvenir albums and another on crop circles.

Of all the many published works, promotional and commercial, produced by Pentagram, the Papers are arguably the one piece that sets the firm apart—an interesting point since Pentagram has made a conscious effort to respect the editorial autonomy of the content and avoid the perception of self-promotion. "Yes, everything we put out is 'sell' in some way, but this is 'sell' in the softest manner," McConnell says. That being the case, Pentagram has demonstrated the effectiveness of soft sell by letting the editorial content of Pentagram Papers communicate the firm's personality—intellectually curious, eclectic, and receptive to things going on in the world—and barely mentioning itself at all.

The Pentagram Papers: 1975 to 2006

There are no rules for the design of the Pentagram Papers, save for their uniform size and the dull gloss black cover with white ruled border. Inside, the design treatment is as individual as the partner who executed it. Despite the seeming lack of design guidelines inside, Pentagram Papers have a consistent feel that makes them recognizable on sight.

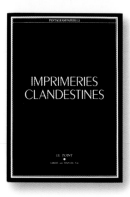

Cultural Phenomena

It takes attaining critical mass, and often the perspective of hindsight, to distinguish a cultural phenomenon from a passing fad. The ordinary objects that rise to that level speak volumes about a culture's values and mores. They are the signatures of an era, a region, a political movement, a vanishing way of life. What makes these objects so fascinating is their larger meaning. A collection of garish 1950s doo-wop motel signs on the New Jersey shore leaves one musing about mid-century ideas of modernity. Tools improvised from recycled parts in embargoed Cuba cause one to marvel over ingenuity in the midst of poverty. Whimsical homemade mailboxes in the Australian Outback encapsulate a resourceful frontier spirit. Seen through the eyes of observant outsiders, these objects enrich our view of the world.

No. 30: **Doo-Wop Commercial Architecture**

Back Story

Partner Michael Bierut and his wife, photographer Dorothy Kresz, who have been vacationing on the Jersey shore since the early '80s, discovered Wildwood while passing through one evening. The place, frozen in time, fascinated Dorothy and she kept returning to the town to photograph its funky motel signs. At a partners' meeting, Bierut screened his wife's photos of Wildwood to provide a funny example of "populist design gone wild." It was such a hit that soon an editor at the *New Yorker* asked to see the photos as a possible accompaniment to a story the magazine was considering on Wildwood. The story never ran, but writer Jonathan van Meter, who also wrote the book *The Last Good Time*, set in Atlantic City, liked what he saw and adapted his article for the introduction to this Pentagram Paper.

NEON-LIT KIDNEY-SHAPED LOW-RENT FLAT-ROOFED DOO-WOP COMMERCIAL ARCHITECTURE

At the southern tip of the Jersey shore is Wildwood, a working-class resort architecturally frozen in the 1950s, with its neon-lit signs and towering plastic palm trees that keep their tropical look even in a blizzard. Post-war prosperity let Americans pile the kids in the car and head off on motor vacations. What better destination than places like nearby Wildwood, with its miles of beaches, boardwalk rides, and motels where you could literally park outside your door?

Few, if any, of the motels in Wildwood were designed by architects, but were copies of buildings seen by developers who wintered in Florida. Given exotic names and themes like Casa Bahama, Pink Champagne, Tahiti, Coral Sands, and Shalimar, these flat-roofed boxy buildings, stuccoed in flamboyant colors and sporting huge neon signs, shouted to be recognized.

But as the decades wore on, the motels became tired relics of another age. In the 1990s, local leaders sought to revitalize the area by calling in urban experts. Instead of spurning the often-boarded-up motels, the experts considered them a treasure—the nation's largest collection of mid-century commercial architecture. Dubbing it "doo-wop" architecture, they urged the town to restore the motels, preserving the authentic flavor of a 1950s blue-collar resort.

ALL THE WAY

At the southernmost tip of New Jersey lies Cape May, a jewel of a place, busy with mid-century Victoriana. The entire city is an historic landmark and, thanks to a preservation movement that began in the early '70s to save Cape May's exemplary turn-of-century architecture, the resort is greatly improving its unparalleled full-year activity base of a thriving 11-month bed and breakfast season. It's small but for a Northeastern beach town with a short summer and a long, cold winter. Cape May is attractive, pretty and prim, pretty with tree-lined streets, wrap-around porches and rocking chairs, antique shops and lively restaurants. Martha Stewart would approve. Just north of Cape May, on a narrow five-mile-long barrier island lies Wildwood. While only a drawbridge away in spiritual and architectural as far one could possibly get from Cape May, Wildwood is an in-your-face urban challenge, place with a bad neighborhood of two bars and nightclubs, drug problems and a 26% unemployment rate. It's a bit gritty and wonderfully tacky, all with neon signs and a street with big plastic palm trees in lieu of a real greenery, like a miniature Manhattan on the beach. Wildwood is a

almost cement and blacktop grid, with avenues all running up and down and short blocks cutting across. The resort there are actually four separate towns: Wildwood, Wildwood Crest, West Wildwood and North Wildwood) has been known over the years mainly for two things: one of the last great honky tonk boardwalks in the country, with six piers and more (and better rides than Disneyland), and the widest beach on the East coast (1800 feet and growing). But only recently has Wildwood become known for its architecture, what some argue is the strongest concentration of mid-century commercial buildings anywhere in the world.

WILDWOOD,

as urban planners and preservationists like to say, has "a story": it's the original 1950s, blue collar resort, and it has remained largely undisturbed for the past thirty years. People use words like "pickled" and "freeze-dried" to describe Wildwood, a fact that the economically battered locals find demoralizing. But for the increasing numbers of curious, urbane outsiders, Wildwood is nothing less than a wonderland of authenticity. It's a place with a soul, and, in an increasingly overplanned and overdesigned world, the fact that urban renewal passed Wildwood by has begun to seem like an incredible blessing.

To understand the uniqueness and importance of Wildwood, one must go back to its beginnings, to the neighboring metropolis Philadelphia, and the birth of working class vacation culture. The great Philadelphian William Sellers, a world premiere manufacturer of machines and the president of the Franklin Institute, ushered in the era of

and separate standardization in the mid 70s, which led to the creation of the Pennsylvania Rail Road, and Philadelphia at least for a time, in the industrial process.

In 1880, Sellers's adopted nephew Taylor, who was working at one of his plants, radically reorganized the management of his uncle's companies, increasing productivity. Taylor then put the benefits on to the worker in the form of attributed salaries. "What Taylor did," writes George Thomas, an architectural historian from Philadelphia who teaches at the University of Pennsylvania, "was solve the Marxist dilemma. The Marxists said religion was the opiate of the masses. Taylor turned them into consumers. That was the great step: by raising wages they promoted labor harmony, and even though the work became numbingly boring, they all looked forward to what they were going to do on the weekend. And this found in these series of working class resorts along the Jersey Shore, Wildwood being the most exemplary. Wildwood represents the world of the empowerment of the worker and the possibilities of those people having the luxury and the spare time and the cash to produce Wildwood." (In January 1998, the Philadelphia Inquirer published a study about urban density in Philadelphia: it turns out, is the 42nd most dense urban center in the country. Wildwood is 43rd.)

Wildwood, like all of the other Jersey Shore towns went through various periods of stagnation and spurts of growth, but it wasn't until the 1950's that it became the resort that it at least physically, it remains today. Post war prosperity sent record numbers of people to the Jersey Shore. In the summer of 1946, vacationers in the region

spent $400 million. 10 years later they spent $1.7 billion. This spike in leisure growth was largely the result of New Jersey's Garden State Parkway, which was completed in 1956.

THE HUGE EXPLOSION

in tourism strained the limits of Wildwood's aging outdated hotels. But because the Parkway development actually began in the late '40s, the-highway-is-coming fever inspired a few enterprising developers to look to the future: The Motel. The product of 20 years of evolution—from tourist camps to cottages to auto camps to motor courts—the modern motel of the 1950's was, in essence, the perfection of a new idea in travel, the motor-vacation, in which the car actually becomes part of the experience, parked, literally, right outside your door. The appeal of the motel has always been its casualness: the exterior circulation of the balcony, the swimming pool as a kind of courtyard onto which all the rooms looked, kitchenettes, maybe a shuffleboard court, maybe a game room, and free ice. No bellhops. No doormen. No room service. No tipping. And, of course, a TV in every room. By 1946, there were 26,000 motels and motor courts in the United States; another 15,000 were built between 1949 and 1952. In the seminal, far-sighted *Learning From Las Vegas*, published in 1972, Robert Venturi, Denise Scott Brown and Steven Izenhour wrote: "The Miami Beach Modern motel on a bleak stretch of highway in Southern Delaware reminds jaded drivers

Tailfin shapes, tropical themes, and bright neon signage beckoned customers along the Jersey shore.

This Paper was titled "Neon-Lit Kidney-Shaped Low-Rent Flat-Roofed Doo-Wop Commercial Architecture" in humorous homage to author Tom Wolfe, who loves to poke fun at artistic pretensions.

These photographs are just a sampling of the two thousand or so scenes that Dorothy Kresz shot of Wildwood and its environs.

No. 21: **Crop Circles**

Crop circles—flattened stalks of grain formed into geometric patterns—have mysteriously appeared in the fields of England for decades. Although scientists from around the world have tried to find a logical explanation for the crop circles, which materialize overnight, no one has come forth with a provable theory. Nobody knows how the circles arrive, who makes them, or how—or what, if anything, they mean. The source of the circles has been attributed to everything from extraterrestrials and military radiation to two elderly men named Doug and Dave. In recent years, crop circles have increased in size, complexity, and frequency of appearance. The smallest are about 25 feet in diameter and some of the larger ones extend to 440 feet. Southern England has reported the largest number of crop circles, although other parts of the world have reported a few of their own. The geometric shapes of the most sophisticated crop circles convey a mathematical elegance that is both awesome and baffling.

Back Story

Michael Glickman, a Pentagram friend, architect, designer, and inventor, is well known among "cerealogists"—people who engage in the study of crop circles. Through Glickman, partner John McConnell saw the work of other cerealogists, primarily Wolfgang Schindler, John Martineau, and John Langrish, who photographed, surveyed, and cataloged crop circles and rendered them into pure graphic forms. What struck McConnell as amazing was the sophistication of the geometric shapes. The confident, elegant lines and increasing variety and invention of the circles won his admiration. Whether done by aliens or earthly creatures, the formations exhibited an intelligent grasp of proportions, symmetry, and construction that deserved to be brought to public attention.

Avebury Trusloe 9 June 1991   East Kennet 27 July 1991

Telegraph Hill 16 June 1990   Longwood Estate 28 June 1990

These drawings of crop circle forms were made by working with site measurements or aerial photographs. When simplified to black-and-white silhouettes, the circles support the belief that they were made by an intelligent being.

Etchilhampton Hill 29 July 1990

Westbury July 1990

Firs Farm 1 August 1991

Hackpen Hill 12 July 1991

West Stowell 3 August 1992

Cerealogists have noted repetitive patterns in the forms although they appear on different farms.

The complexity, precision, and scale of the forms have produced many theories but no logical explanation.

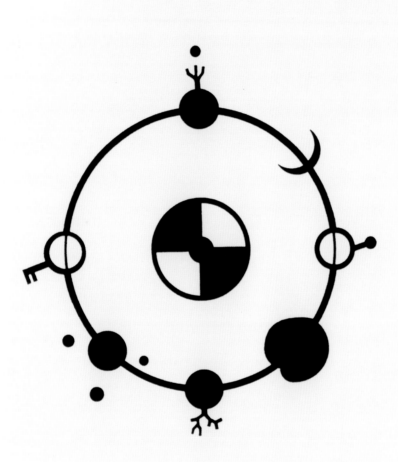

Silbury 17 August 1992

No. 34: **Monografías**

Back Story

While on a trip to Mexico, New York–based photographer Grant Delin became enchanted with *monografías* and brought several home with him. He showed them to Pentagram partner Michael Bierut, who says he was drawn to them "not just for their folkloric charm, but because they were an interesting example of information design—concise, wordless, and sometimes comic in their vast sweep and determination to reduce a vast amount of information into a few images." Graphic designer Armin Vit was enlisted to write his recollections of the *monografías* that he used as a boy growing up in Mexico City.

As every Mexican schoolchild knows, *monografías* are colorfully illustrated teaching aids available on an encyclopedic range of subjects. Costing about 2.50 pesos (or U.S. 25 cents), each *monografía* features a similar design. The front side presents about sixteen illustrations, set on a tight grid, that display various aspects of a single topic—such as corn and its derivatives, the feudal age, or evolution. The back side consists of boxed text, set on the same grid, that diligently reports on the corresponding image on the front. Drawn by unidentified artists, the illustrations tend to be crudely realistic and anatomically correct.

The accompanying text makes no literary pretense but is purely informational and dryly written. Not required to adhere to educational standards, the *monografías*, produced by privately owned companies, freely, and sometimes inaccurately, interpret historic events, political movements, and natural facts. Still, children embrace them, and even shy teenagers have found value in *monografías* on topics like sexual reproductive organs.

In the opening essay, Mexico City–born graphic designer Armin Vit recalls how, as an eight-year-old, one of his most memorable moments was the excitement of walking to the neighborhood *papelería* with his mother to buy his first *monografía*, on prehistoric animals.

PRIMATES (MONOS)

EPSA No. 399

Mandril / Ateles / Macaco / Seminopiteco

Colobo / Gorila / Titi / Babuino

Gibón / Mono diana / Nasica / Chimpancé

Cinocéfalo / Mono araña / Orangután / Mono de la India

SISTEMA SOLAR

ASTEROIDES

MERCURIO

...CIONES BOB, S.A. M-107

Español con Mora / Mulata

...con Mulata / ...Lobo

Canbujo con India / Sanbaigo

Sanbaigo con Loba / Calpamulato

Calpamulato con Canbuja / Tente en el Aire

Tente en el Aire con Mulata / Noteentiendo

Noteentiendo con India / Tornaatras

MONOGRAFÍAS

INFORMATION DESIGN
FOR THE
MEXICAN SCHOOLROOM

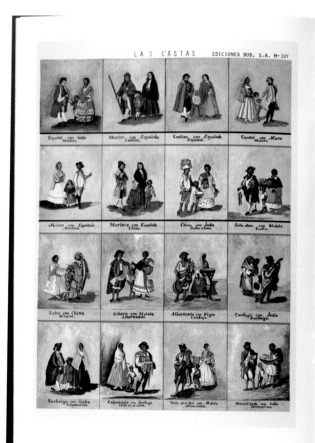

Monografía illustrations run the gamut from no-nonsense realism to romanticized interpretations. Michael Bierut turned the *monografía* drawing of a cow into a visual pun by featuring half on the inside front cover and the other half on the back.

EL ARCO IRIS (FENOMENO LUMINOSO)

VIBRACIONES EN LA CORTEZA TERRESTRE (TERREMOTOS)

LOS COMETAS (FENOMENOS CELESTES)

ERUPCION VOLCANICA

LA TROMBA (FENOMENO MARITIMO)

ECLIPSE LUNAR

ECLIPSE SOLAR

TEMPESTAD EN EL MAR

LOS GRANDES "DESIERTOS"

LA AURORA BOREAL

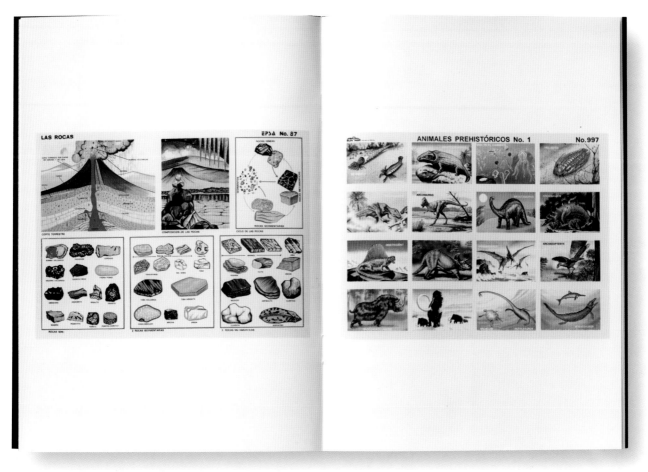

LAS ROCAS

EPSA No. 87

ANIMALES PREHISTÓRICOS No. 1 No.997

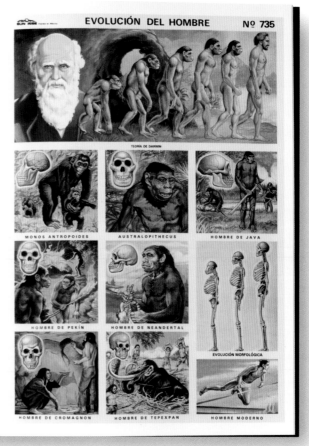

Monografías are available on every subject, including alcoholism, aviation, primates, human evolution, and the moon.

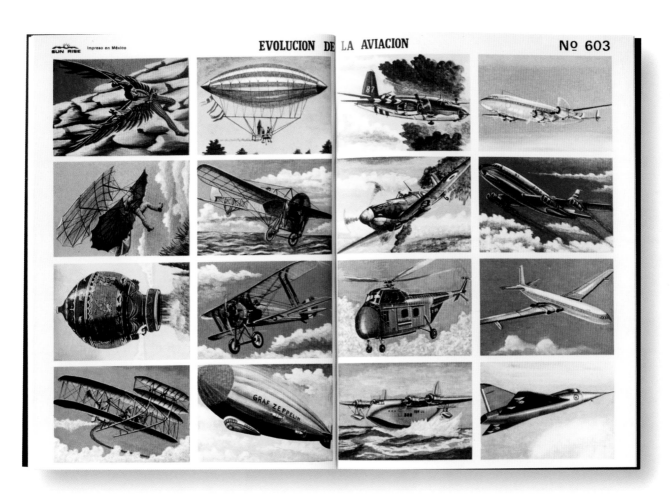

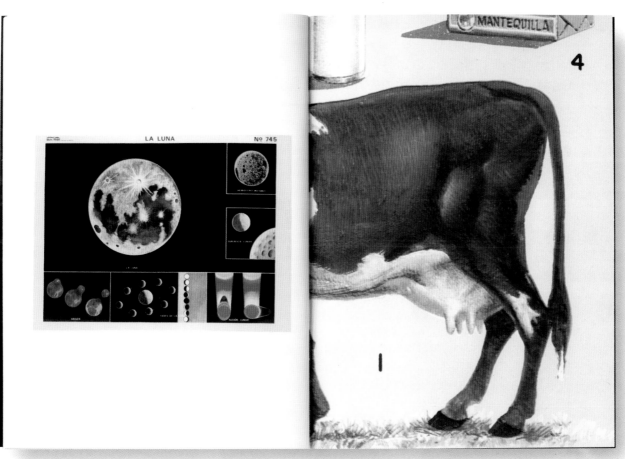

No. 32: **No Waste**

From colleagues in his native Spain, partner Fernando Gutiérrez says he kept hearing about the amazing work being done by progressive young Cuban artists, and went to Havana to see for himself. Gutiérrez found the artists' techniques and expressiveness inspirational, but even more fascinating to him was an exhibition of *objetos de la necesidad*, documented and produced by the Laboratorio de Creación Maldeojo. To feature the recycled items in a Pentagram Paper, Gutiérrez, who had earlier served as art director of Benetton's *Colors* magazine, enlisted Alex Marashian, then editor-in-chief of *Colors*, to write an introduction. A Californian living in Rome, Marashian had previously produced an entire issue of *Colors* on a Cuban town called Baracoa.

With the collapse of the Soviet Union and its satellite states in the early 1990s, Cuba entered a period of severe economic crisis and deprivation. During what is referred to, both officially and popularly, as the "special period," Cubans turned to alternative sources of energy, transport, and most basic commodities. Homemade and handmade objects, some designed to meet basic needs and others to re-create lost comforts, proliferated. Cobbled together from whatever materials were available, these everyday things displayed resourceful ingenuity. Most were recycled from broken-down parts, reincarnated into new things, and salvaged again for parts when that item wore out. Unlike native crafts made by aboriginal cultures, most of the improvised objects, such as sunglasses and lamps, were patterned after modern products, substituting materials to imitate what was not available. The result was something humble yet familiar, crude yet occasionally stylish.

The photographing of these jury-rigged objects was undertaken in the mid-1990s by Ernesto Aroza, a member of the Laboratorio de Creación Maldeojo, a creative cooperative founded in Havana.

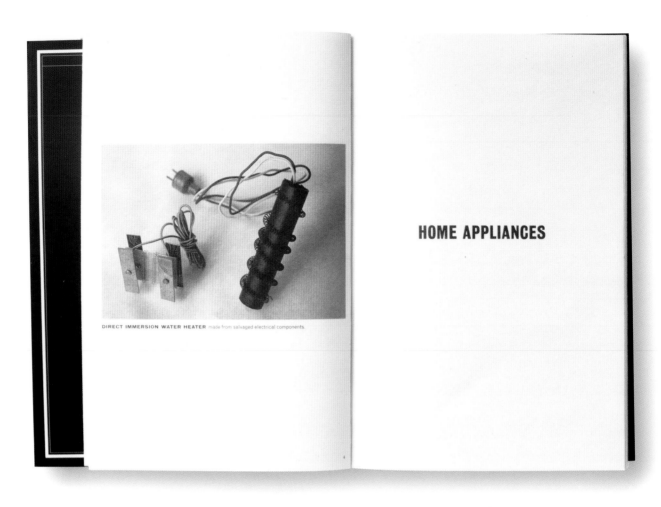

DIRECT IMMERSION WATER HEATER made from salvaged electrical components.

HOME APPLIANCES

SPOON FENCE made with discarded aluminum sheets from eating utensils factory.

LAMP made from glass goblet, toy marbles and pieces of acrylic.

Designed to echo the humbleness of the objects shown, this Pentagram Paper was printed on coarse recycled paper with a brown cardboard inner cover peeking through the die-cut stenciled book title.

PEDAL-PROPELLED VEHICLE made by driver who had no automobile license.

22

TAXI SIGN made from plastic bottle and illuminated at night by internal light bulb.

23

WASHING MACHINE made by attaching Soviet washing machine components to cement sink.

48

WASHING LINE made from nylon candy wraps.

49

RECYCLED KITCHENWARE made by mixing plastics from various sources.

11

PENCIL RAZOR used by soldiers and in some rural areas.

44

HYGIENE

Over a three-year period, filmmaker and poet Nelson Rossell and designers Ernesto Oroza and Fabian Martinez of the Laboratorio de Creación Maldeojo traveled throughout Cuba in search of ingenious objects made from recycled parts.

TELEVISION made with components from computer monitor and various TV sets.

FURNITURE

HANDBAG made from nylon threads found in medical packaging.

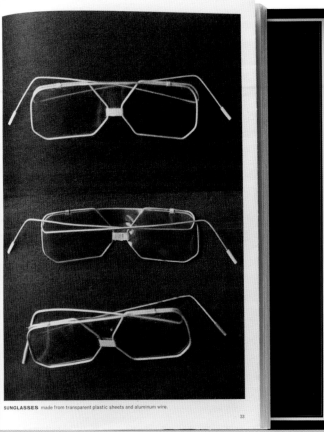

SUNGLASSES made from transparent plastic sheets and aluminum wire.

No. 31: **Hinagata: Kimono Pattern Books**

Back Story

While browsing the booths at an antiquarian book fair, partner Kit Hinrichs happened upon two oversized nineteenth-century books with brush-painted Japanese calligraphy on their covers and delicately hand-painted block prints of kimonos inside. The books had no words inside, just pages of pictures of kimonos. Hinrichs' search for what he had acquired led him to seek out Yoshiko I. Wada, a fellow at the Center for Japanese Studies, University of California, Berkeley, and an independent scholar specializing in Japanese textiles. Writer Delphine Hirasuna conducted lengthy interviews with Wada to learn how these kimono pattern books were used.

As early as the seventeenth century, the leading kimono merchant houses in Japan dictated kimono fashion by producing pattern books, called *hinagata*, that were purchased by textile dyers, manufacturers, and kimono sellers to use as design references. The books themselves were exquisite works of art—block-printed and hand-painted in delicate colors to communicate the subtle beauty of the finished products.

A precursor to contemporary fashion magazines, *hinagata* were intended to display the kimono designs to best advantage to generate desire for the custom-made robes, which at that point were nothing more than a raw bolt of unprinted silk.

The oldest-known pattern book was published in 1667 as a two-volume set and contained two hundred kimono designs block-printed in black ink. Over the next 150 years, some 180 *hinagata* were published in the ancient imperial capital of Kyoto, giving birth to a thriving publishing industry as well as the textile weaving and dyeing trade. Despite the artistry displayed in the *hinagata*, the designers remained anonymous craftspeople hired to put together what was essentially an order catalog.

ILLUSTRATOR UNKNOWN

To evoke a sense of place and time, the caption copy ran vertically on the page in a Japanese calligraphic manner. A tactile, uncoated paper with a French fold binding enhanced the period feeling.

For all its stylized sumptuousness, the Japanese *kimono* (which means "wearable object") is simply constructed. Unlike Western apparel, it has no tucks, pleats, buttons, zippers or contoured shape. Made from a single bolt of cloth (14 inches x 12 yards), the T-shaped garment (a style previously known in Japan as *kosode*) retains the integrity of the original bolt design. Essentially, the robe is pieced from two lengths of fabric draped over the shoulders and sewn together at the back and sides, and two shorter lengths attached to form sleeves. The basic cut and shape of kimonos are the same for male and female, young and old, rich and poor. What individualizes one kimono from another is the material, weave, color and decorative pattern. Customers select a bolt of undyed cloth, the motif, color and sometimes the lining material and the *obi* sash to go with it to achieve the specific look they have in mind.

From as early as the 17th century, the leading kimono merchant houses would dictate kimono fashion by producing pattern books that were purchased by textile dyers, manufacturers and kimono sellers to use

THROUGH THE LATE EDO PERIOD (CIRCA 1800–67), KIMONO MERCHANTS WOULD VISIT THE HOMES OF WEALTHY PATRONS TO DISPLAY THEIR FINERIES. THIS WOOD-BLOCK PRINT SHOWS A MERCHANT CALLING ON A GEISHA HOUSE, WHERE HE PRESENTS A BOOK OF KIMONO PATTERNS (HINAKATA-BON) AND A BOLT OF SILK. THE WOMAN IN BACK IS EXAMINING A BROCADED OBI (SASH).

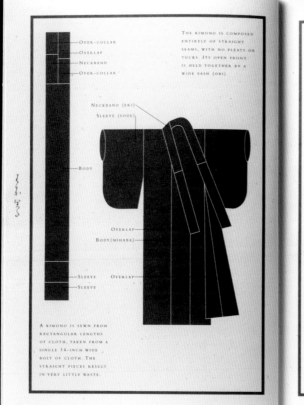

OVER-COLLAR
OVERLAP
NECKBAND
OVER-COLLAR

NECKBAND (ERI)
SLEEVE (SODE)

BODY

OVERLAP
BODY (MIHADA)

SLEEVE   OVERLAP
SLEEVE

THE KIMONO IS COMPOSED ENTIRELY OF STRAIGHT SEAMS, WITH NO PLEATS OR TUCKS. ITS OPEN FRONT IS HELD TOGETHER BY A WIDE SASH (OBI).

A KIMONO IS SEWN FROM RECTANGULAR LENGTHS OF CLOTH, TAKEN FROM A SINGLE 14-INCH WIDE BOLT OF CLOTH. THE STRAIGHT PIECES RESULT IN VERY LITTLE WASTE.

as design references. *On-hiinakata*, the oldest known pattern book, was published in 1667 as a two-volume set, containing 200 kimono designs block-printed in black ink. Over the next 150 years, some 180 pattern books were published in the ancient Imperial capital of Kyoto, giving birth to a thriving publishing industry and textile weaving and dyeing trade.

For the most part, the artists who created the kimono designs remained anonymous – although pattern books occasionally credited the pattern maker and the technical coordinator for dyeing. A rare exception is Hishikawa Moronobu (1618 – 1694) who founded the *Ukiyo-e* school of block printing. Born into a respected Kyoto fabric dyeing and textile design family, Moronobu honed his skill as a painter and printmaker while drawing kimono patterns. He continued to design patterns for wealthy patrons even in his later years.

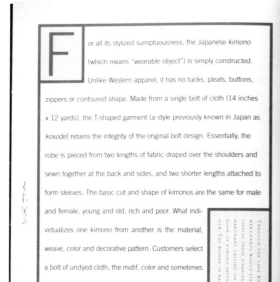

FROM THE 17TH CENTURY TO THE MEIJI ERA, PATTERN BOOKS SERVED THE FUNCTION OF FASHION MAGAZINES. THIS BOOK FROM 1691 SHOWS A WELL-KNOWN KABUKI ACTOR OF THE DAY MODELING A KIMONO, SHOWN IN FULL VIEW ABOVE. THE WORDS DESCRIBE SUGGESTED COLORS FOR THE FLOWERS.

In addition to describing the history and making of kimonos, the Pentagram Paper showed elegantly hand-painted drawings of bridal underkimono and print patterns offered by one nineteenth-century kimono cloth maker.

ELABORATE BRIDAL UNDERKIMONO DESIGNS INCOR-
PORATE A WIDE RANGE OF ARTISTIC TECHNIQUES
FROM YUZEN (PASTE-RESIST) TO SHIBORI (TIE-DYE).

THIS BRIDAL UNDERKIMONO IS DECORATED WITH
WISTERIA, CHRYSANTHEMUMS AND WATER PLANTS.

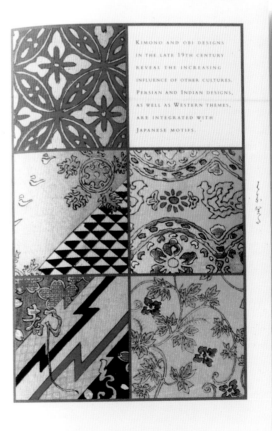

KIMONO AND OBI DESIGNS
IN THE LATE 19TH CENTURY
REVEAL THE INCREASING
INFLUENCE OF OTHER CULTURES.
PERSIAN AND INDIAN DESIGNS,
AS WELL AS WESTERN THEMES,
ARE INTEGRATED WITH
JAPANESE MOTIFS.

No. 10: **1211 North LaSalle**

Commissioned to give the drab facade of a Chicago apartment building the look of architectural importance, artist Richard Haas set about painting a trompe l'oeil mural. Swiss-born photographer François Robert, whose studio was nearby, followed the progress, diligently recording the step-by-step transformation on film over a ninety-day period.

For Haas, the challenge was to aesthetically enhance three unadorned exterior walls that were left exposed after a nearby demolition. His solution was to create a faux facade that took as its major influence the Chicago School of Architecture and some references to the Italian 1920s eclectic style. On the north and south faces, he painted ten stories of large rectangular windows. Reflected in the "glass" were Chicago skyscrapers that were designed for a 1922 *Chicago Tribune* competition, but never built. On the east side of the building, Haas painted Chicago bay windows in keeping with the city's most successful architectural period, and for the south base, he painted a decorated arch à la architect Louis Sullivan. The completed murals looked so realistic that one woman insisted on viewing the model apartment with bay windows.

monce | St
Hammond
Tell Ct.
Black
Eugenie | St.
T Starr St. St. H
Ave. St.
A R K
XVII
St.
Burton Pl.
St.
Church
Sedgwick
Hurlbut
St.
St. St.
Schiller
Siegel St
Bank
Heine
Goethe
St.
Scott
Granger St
D E
St.
St. St. St.
St.
Cedar S
St. St.
Hill St.
Maple St. Bellevue Pl.
Wendell St.
XIX St.
VIII
Whiting St. LaFayette Pl. Walton Pl
White St. WAS Delaware St.
NGTON SQ
Brewer
Townsend
Sedgwick
Chestnut St. St. St
Chestnut
Pearson
Pearson St. St.
Superior
Sedgwick
urton WATE
St. St.

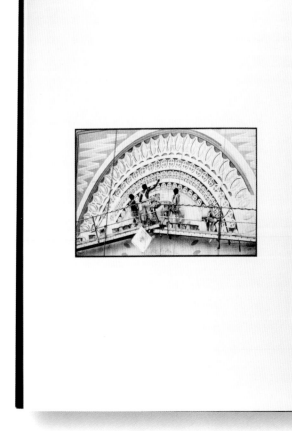

Photographer François Robert went to 1211 North LaSalle every day to record Richard Haas' progress. Robert envisioned creating a photo flipbook, but instead worked with a filmmaker to transform the stills into a three-minute time-lapse film.

No. 27: **Nifty Places: The Australian Rural Mailbox**

Back Story

While on a lecture tour of Australia, partner David Hillman was hosted at one seminar by Cal Swann, professor of design at Curtin University in Perth. Swann had been head of graphic design at Saint Martin's School of Art in London before accepting a position at the University of South Australia in 1989. As an immigrant to Australia, Swann viewed everyday sights from an outsider's perspective, and was particularly struck by the creativity of the homemade mailboxes that stood in the middle of nowhere in the Outback. Over the years, he had photographed them. He showed his collection to Hillman, who asked if he could reprint them as a Pentagram Paper.

"One of the most visible demonstrations of Aussie individuality and inventiveness, bordering on art on the one hand and environmental vandalism on the other, is the rural mailbox," observes Cal Swann, a British designer who moved to western Australia in 1989 and provided the content for this edition of the Pentagram Papers. These icons of the Outback are made from all kinds of recycled materials, with old milk churns, oil drums, and big plastic jugs being the most popular. Any waterproof depository that can be propped up on a pole will do. The one thing they are not is store-bought and fancy. Undoubtedly, the early settlers devised their own makeshift mailboxes out of practical necessity, but their descendants have carried on the tradition out of a gleeful respect for native ingenuity. As pragmatic and humble as these mailboxes are, many owners seize the opportunity to express their individuality and whimsy and give a chuckle or a pause to occasional travelers who pass by.

45c

AUSTRALIA

Outback Services

2001

Some areas of the Australian Outback are so remote and inaccessible that mail is delivered by plane. In these isolated locations, so many people shop by mail order that large receptacles are chosen for mailboxes to hold package deliveries.

Readily available oil drums, milk cans, and plastic jugs provide waterproof qualities that are ideal for mailboxes. Jugs and drums are easy to prop up on wooden posts or suspend from a pole or tree limb.

organisation which had joined and cheekily upstaged the existing women's suffrage movement centred around Mrs Millicent Garrett Fawcett's National Union of Women's Suffrage Societies, a lady-like and law-abiding organisation. The Suffragettes' finances and organisation were impressive - within five years of arriving in London they raised the modern equivalent of three million pounds. Members would buy the three colour sashes emblazoned with Votes for Women; trim their hats and boaters with purple, white and green ribbon; could buy canvas satchels for selling the weekly newspapers *Votes For Women* and *The Suffragette*; wore badges and brooches. The wealthy suffragette could buy tea-gowns in the three colours, accessorised with Suffragette Jewellery, say a gold pendant set with emeralds, pearls and amethysts specially made by Mappin and Webb; drive a motor car painted and upholstered in these colours, or ride one of the new Safety Bicycles whose chain-guard was decorated with the suffragette logo of an angel blowing a bugle for freedom, designed by Sylvia Pankhurst. Suffragettes made birthday and Christmas cakes iced in the three colours and advertised them in the classified columns of their newspapers.

VOTES FOR WOMEN

Women's Coronation

PROCESSION

(Five miles long).

Saturday, June 17th,

START 5.30 P.M.

Route via:—TRAFALGAR SQUARE, PALL MALL, PICCADILLY, KNIGHTSBRIDGE.

70 BANDS!
1,000 BANNERS!

This Pentagram Paper was printed as an eight-panel accordion-fold booklet, inserted inside the black cover. The single-side

Purple, White and Green

A Victorian tinsel bearing a photograph of Mrs Pankhurst (courtesy of Richard Pankhurst)

Suffragette prisoners who went on hunger strike and were force fed were awarded this medal

Founded in Manchester in 1903 by the Pankhurst family, Mrs Emmeline Pankhurst and her daughters Christabel and Sylvia, the Women's Social and Political Union moved to London in 1906. They arrived with the nickname Suffragettes which had been given to them by *The Daily Mail*, already shocked by their tactics. They lived up to their slogan 'Deeds Not Words', so their presence on the political scene was soon felt. Operating from two small rooms at number 4 Clement's Inn, The Strand, they became the hub of a nationwide campaign to persuade or force the Liberal Government to give women the vote. Within eighteen months of their arrival in London the purple, white and green colour scheme was worn. Their weekly newspaper *Votes For Women* explained the choice of colours: "Purple as every-one knows is the royal colour. It stands for the royal blood that runs in the veins of every Suffragette, the instinct of freedom and dignity... white stands for purity in private and public life... green is the colour of hope and the emblem of spring."

The women who wore these colours were displaying their allegiance to this new and daring

No. 19: **Purple, White and Green**

Back Story

For partner John McConnell, the suffragettes were among the savviest lobbyists of the twentieth century. "What interested me was that they invented a graphic identity for their cause," he says. "They chose colors to represent themselves; adopted a slogan; printed a lot of pamphlets, posters, and banners; and staged publicity-grabbing events. Design was used as a central device in raising the visibility of their campaign." Most of the items shown in the Pentagram Paper came from the Museum of London's collection of suffragette material.

Purple, white, and green had unique meaning in early twentieth-century England because they were the colors of the Women's Social and Political Union, founded in 1903 by Mrs. Emmeline Pankhurst and her daughters, Christabel and Sylvia. Adopting the slogan "Deeds, Not Words," these suffragettes, as the *Daily Mail* labeled them, were organized, militant, and bold. They staged boycotts and hunger strikes and picketed legislators to win women the vote. They also knew how to elevate their public visibility by linking purple, white, and green with their cause. The suffragette newspaper *Votes for Women* explained that each color was rife with meaning. "Purple as everyone knows is the royal colour. It stands for the royal blood that runs in the veins of every suffragette, the instinct of freedom and dignity . . . white stands for purity in private and public life . . . green is the colour of hope and the emblem of spring."

Movement sympathizers embraced this symbolism, adopting the colors for everything from clothing and jewelry to sashes, hat ribbons, and greeting cards. The ubiquitous sight of these colors convinced Parliament that there was a groundswell of support, and in 1918, it voted to give women in Britain the vote.

...wielded a direct or
...n's Social and Political
...d or moral. It was the
...erchandise its message
...going, imaginative and
...one it better.

A pretty tin badge designed by Sylvia Pankhurst, courtesy of Richard Pankhurst

A beaded glass necklace

Laurence Housman's anti Anti Suffrage Alphabet Book of 1912, courtesy of the Housman Estate, Jonathan Cape Publishers

A detail of purple, white and green satin

VOTES FOR WOMEN.

B is the Brute
who beats his wife.
Physical Force is the
rule of life:
In Church & State, in Home & School
Physical Force is the way to rule.

Freedom and women's suffrage were synonymous for suffragettes

Working-class members could afford to buy penny tin badges and postcards of their heroines, the star personalities like Mrs Pankhurst and her daughter Christabel and the mill-girl Annie Kenney. The Women's Coronation Procession of June 17th 1911, advertised well in advance, enabled manufacturers and retailers to profit from this event. 'White Attire for Processional Wear', floral bouquets in purple, white and green, and Hygiama food tablets, a 'snack for the route' were some of the products. The slogan 'Votes for Women' was merchandised vigorously and successfully. 'Votes for Women' handkerchiefs, soap, chocolate, marmalade, tea and cigarettes were sold at The Woman's Press, 156 Charing Cross Road and at about twenty Women's Social and Political Union shops in London and the United Kingdom. Card games like 'Panko', 'The Game of Suffragette' and a puzzle called 'Suffragettes In and Out of Prison' were Christmas stocking-fillers. Suffragettes would send each other purple, white and green Votes for Women Christmas cards, calendars and greetings cards. One could buy lace tablecloths with suffragettes holding placards bearing the initials V.F.W. and being chased by portly police constables worked into the lace.

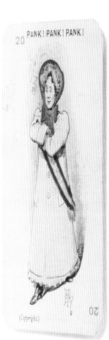

Most of the items produced
indirect benefit for the Wom
Union, be it financial, politic
first political organisation to r
and image in such a thorough
successful way. No one has c

ress run gave readers an at-a-glance look at the variety of things made with the suffragettes' purple, white, and green colors.

No. 24: **The Arms of Paris**

The important role that the River Seine played in the commerce and defense of Paris for more than seven hundred years is reflected in the city's coat of arms—a boat with billowing sails floating along the water. Paris originally developed on two islands, the Ile de la Cité and the Ile Saint-Louis, in the middle of the river, before extending onto the right and left banks. Boats supplied all of the inhabitants' necessities. An obvious symbol for the city's dominant trade, the riverboat was adopted by a thirteenth-century salt company as a seal for its bills of sale. City fathers appropriated the emblem, making it the coat of arms for Paris, but not before converting the modest boat into a majestic high-board vessel. The fact that such a boat could not have passed under the low bridges of Paris did not deter them from turning the sails into billowing towers. In 1699, the emblem was formally registered in the *Armorial Général*, the official book of all coats of arms. Although the design has gone through many iterations, the emblem and accompanying motto, "She floats but she does not sink," have remained constant over the centuries.

The Arms of Paris

Since Paris was no more
than two islands in the River Seine,
its emblem has been a boat.
Over hundreds of years
it has appeared
in countless manifestations.
Photographer Claude Bestel
has recorded the
extraordinary variety to be found
throughout the city.

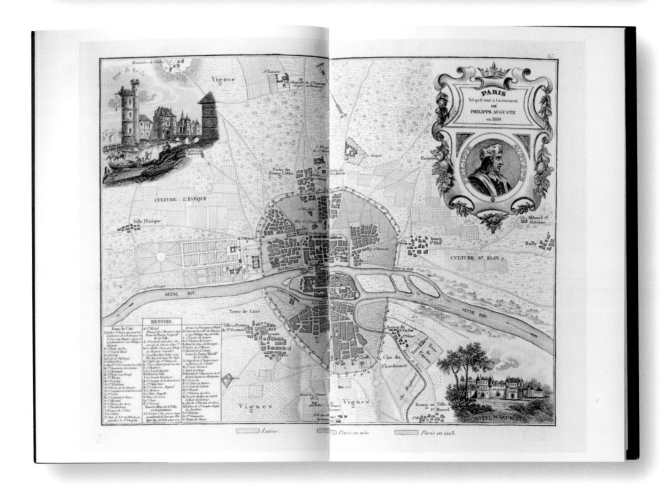

Surprisingly, the sailboat emblem of Paris is often overlooked despite its omnipresence on hundreds of public buildings.

Opéra, rue Auber

Ventilation column on the corner of rue de Rivoli

Young girl's school, rue Vicq

Girl's school, rue Dupleix

North pillar of the Eiffel Tower

Savings bank, rue Cler

Gare d'Austerlitz metro station

The townhall, 5ème arrondissement

The Parisian coat of arms has been rendered in virtually every material, including wrought iron, brick, marble, mosaic tile, and plaster. The oars visible on many of these boats date the craft to a time when river boats were the dominant vehicle for trade.

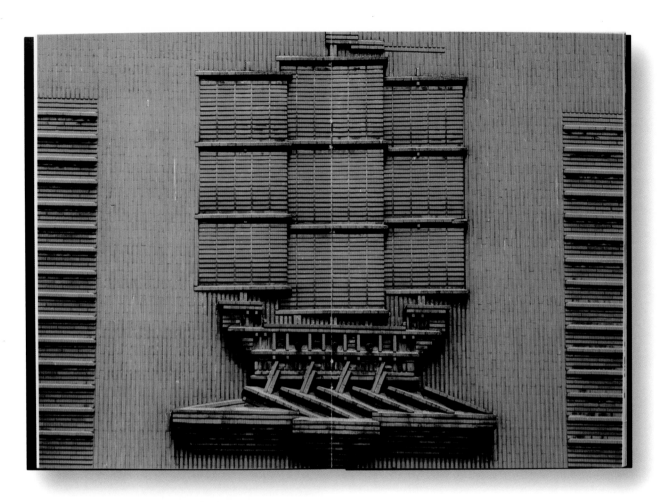

Official sign, rue Saint-Martin

Right: Official townhall stamp, 7ème arrondissement
Left: Police alarm, rue Geoffroy St. Hilaire
Following page: Collège Jean Perrin , rue Eugène Reisz

No. 1: **ABC: A Dictionary of Graphic Clichés**

Back Story

Designer and illustrator Philip Thompson, who had been a classmate of partner Alan Fletcher at the Central School of Art and Design, was a frequent visitor to Pentagram's London office. On one visit, he showed the London partners a draft of *A Dictionary of Graphic Clichés*, a book he was compiling with designer Peter Davenport, and lamented that they were having trouble finding a publisher. Recognizing the undertaking as a valuable resource, partners John McConnell and Colin Forbes decided the dictionary was just the kind of work that they wanted to bring to light in the Pentagram Papers. The first Pentagram Paper presented the A-B-C portion of the dictionary, which was subsequently published in full by Palgrave Macmillan under the title *Dictionary of Graphic Images*.

Graphic cliché is not a derogatory term. Although it suggests frequent use, the images are far from hackneyed. So say designer/illustrator Philip Thompson and designer Peter Davenport, who compiled *A Dictionary of Graphic Clichés*: "Graphic design is a language. Like other languages, it has a vocabulary, grammar, syntax, rhetoric . . . and clichés."

Universally understood in a culture, and sometimes worldwide, graphic clichés allow designers, art directors, and illustrators to "speak" in a kind of visual shorthand language. The Dictionary offers an instructive guide for professionals. For instance—"Blackboard: A natural graphic field with its accompanying chalk marks giving a feeling of immediacy. It often has an educational reference and occasionally a 'spelling it out' connotation, as in the presentation of facts of national importance." "Blackmail lettering: A collage of lettering where each character is cut from a different source and pasted down. . . . " Each graphic cliché is accompanied by an example of use, thus allowing the Dictionary to "show that the wit and personality of the designer can redeem the most overworked raw material, revealing truths as if for the first time."

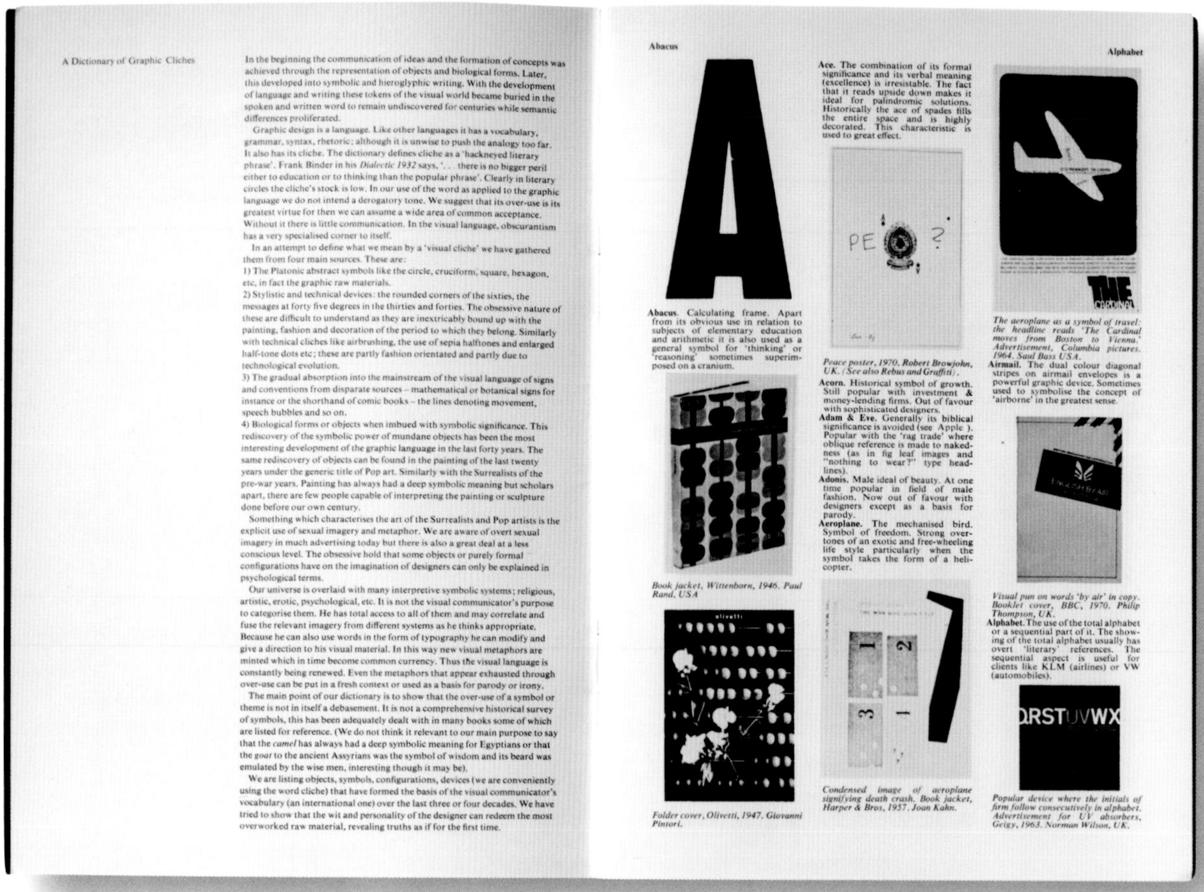

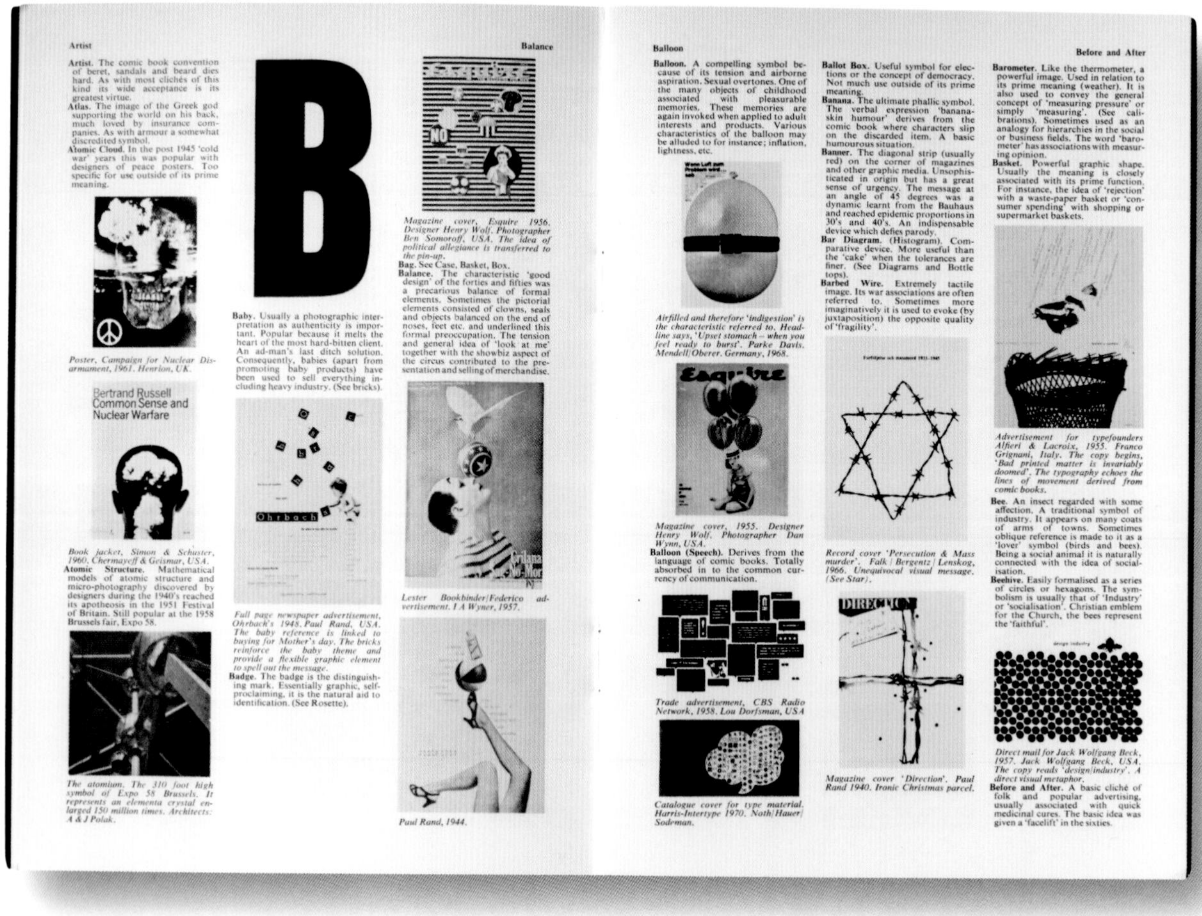

In the beginning the communication of ideas and the formation of concepts was achieved through the representation of objects and biological forms. Later, this developed into symbolic and hieroglyphic writing. With the development of language and writing these tokens of the visual world became buried in the spoken and written word to remain undiscovered for centuries while semantic differences proliferated.

Graphic design is a language. Like other languages it has a vocabulary, grammar, syntax, rhetoric; although it is unwise to push the analogy too far. Also has its cliche. The dictionary defines cliche as a 'hackneyed literary phrase'. Frank Binder in his *Dialectic 1932* says, '. . . there is no bigger peril either to education or to thinking than the popular phrase'. Clearly in literary circles the cliche's stock is low. In our use of the word as applied to the graphic language we do not intend a derogatory tone. We suggest that its over-use is its greatest virtue for then we can assume a wide area of common acceptance. Without it there is little communication. In the visual language, obscurantism has a very specialised corner to itself.

In an attempt to define what we mean by a 'visual cliche' we have gathered them from four main sources. These are:
1) The Platonic abstract symbols like the circle, cruciform, square, hexagon, etc, in fact the graphic raw materials.
2) Stylistic and technical devices: the rounded corners of the sixties, the messages at forty five degrees in the thirties and forties. The obsessive nature of these are difficult to understand as they are inextricably bound up with the painting, fashion and decoration of the period to which they belong. Similarly with technical cliches like airbrushing, the use of sepia halftones and enlarged half-tone dots etc; these are partly fashion orientated and partly due to technological evolution.
3) The gradual absorption into the mainstream of the visual language of signs and conventions from disparate sources – mathematical or botanical signs for instance or the shorthand of comic books – the lines denoting movement, speech bubbles and so on.
4) Biological forms or objects when imbued with symbolic significance. This rediscovery of the symbolic power of mundane objects has been the most interesting development of the graphic language in the last forty years. The same rediscovery of objects can be found in the painting of the last twenty years under the generic title of Pop art. Similarly with the Surrealists of the pre-war years. Painting has always had a deep symbolic meaning but scholars apart, there are few people capable of interpreting the painting or sculpture done before our own century.

Something which characterises the art of the Surrealists and Pop artists is the explicit use of sexual imagery and metaphor. We are aware of overt sexual imagery in much advertising today but there is also a great deal at a less conscious level. The obsessive hold that some objects or purely formal configurations have on the imagination of designers can only be explained in psychological terms.

Our universe is overlaid with many interpretive symbolic systems; religious, artistic, erotic, psychological, etc. It is not the visual communicator's purpose to categorise them. He has total access to all of them and may correlate and fuse the relevant imagery from different systems as he thinks appropriate. Because he can also use words in the form of typography he can modify and give a direction to his visual material. In this way new visual metaphors are minted which in time become common currency. Thus the visual language is constantly being renewed. Even the metaphors that appear exhausted through over-use can be put in a fresh context or used as a basis for parody or irony.

The main point of our dictionary is to show that the over-use of a symbol or theme is not in itself a debasement. It is not a comprehensive historical survey of symbols, this has been adequately dealt with in many books some of which are listed for reference. (We do not think it relevant to our main purpose to say that the *camel* has always had a deep symbolic meaning for Egyptians or that the *goat* to the ancient Assyrians was the symbol of wisdom and its beard was emulated by the wise men, interesting though it may be).

We are listing objects, symbols, configurations, devices (we are conveniently using the word cliche) that have formed the basis of the visual communicator's vocabulary (an international one) over the last three or four decades. We have tried to show that the wit and personality of the designer can redeem the most overworked raw material, revealing truths as if for the first time.

Abacus. Calculating frame. Apart from its obvious use in relation to subjects of elementary education and arithmetic it is also used as a general symbol for 'thinking' or 'reasoning' sometimes superimposed on a cranium.

Peace poster, 1970. Robert Browjohn, UK. (See also Rebus and Graffiti).

Acorn. Historical symbol of growth. Still popular with investment & money-lending firms. Out of favour with sophisticated designers.
Adam & Eve. Generally its biblical significance is avoided (see Apple). Popular with the 'rag trade' where oblique reference is made to nakedness (as in fig leaf images and "nothing to wear?" type headlines).
Adonis. Male ideal of beauty. At one time popular in field of male fashion. Now out of favour with designers except as a basis for parody.
Aeroplane. The mechanised bird. Symbol of freedom. Strong overtones of an exotic and free-wheeling life style particularly when the symbol takes the form of a helicopter.

Condensed image of aeroplane signifying death crash. Book jacket, Harper & Bros, 1957. Joan Kahn.

Book jacket, Wittenborn, 1946. Paul Rand, USA

Folder cover, Olivetti, 1947. Giovanni Pintori.

Ace. The combination of its formal significance and its verbal meaning 'excellence' is irresistible. The fact that it reads upside down makes it ideal for palindromic solutions. Historically the ace of spades fills the entire space and is highly decorated. This characteristic is used to great effect.

The aeroplane as a symbol of travel: the headline reads 'The Cardinal moves from Boston to Vienna.' Advertisement, Columbia pictures, 1964. Saul Bass USA.
Airmail. The dual colour diagonal stripes on airmail envelopes is a powerful graphic device. Sometimes used to symbolise the concept of 'airborne' in the greatest sense.

Visual pun on words 'by air' in copy. Booklet cover, BBC, 1970. Philip Thompson, UK.
Alphabet. The use of the total alphabet or a sequential part of it. The showing of the total alphabet usually has overt 'literary' references. The sequential aspect is useful for clients like KLM (airlines) or VW (automobiles).

Popular device where the initials of firm follow consecutively in alphabet. Advertisement for UV absorbers, Geigy, 1965. Norman Wilson, UK.

Artist. The comic book convention of beret, sandals and beard dies hard. As with most cliches of this kind its wide acceptance is its greatest virtue.
Atlas. The image of the Greek god supporting the world on his back, much loved by insurance companies. As with armour a somewhat discredited symbol.
Atomic Cloud. In the post 1945 'cold war' years this was popular with designers of peace posters. Too specific for use outside of its prime meaning.

Poster, Campaign for Nuclear Disarmament, 1961. Hendon, UK.

Book jacket, Simon & Schuster, 1960. Chermayeff & Geismar, USA.
Atomic Structure. Mathematical models of atomic structure and micro-photography discovered by designers during the 1940's reached its apotheosis in the 1951 Festival of Britain. Still popular at the 1958 Brussels fair, Expo 58.

The atomium. The 310 foot high symbol of Expo 58 Brussels. It represents an elementa crystal enlarged 150 million times. Architects: A & J Polak.

Baby. Usually a photographic interpretation as authenticity is important. Popular because it melts the heart of the most hard-bitten client. An ad-man's last ditch solution. Consequently, babies (apart from promoting baby products) have been used to sell everything including heavy industry. (See bricks).

Full page newspaper advertisement, Ohrbach's 1948. Paul Rand, USA. The baby reference is linked to buying for Mother's day. The bricks reinforce the baby theme and provide a flexible graphic element to spell out the message.
Badge. The badge is the distinguishing mark. Essentially graphic, self-proclaiming, it is the natural aid to identification. (See Rosette).

Magazine cover, Esquire 1956. Designer Henry Wolf. Photographer Ben Somoroff, USA. The idea of political allegiance is transferred to the pin-up.
Bag. See Case, Basket, Box.
Balance. The characteristic 'good design' of the forties and fifties was a precarious balance of graphic elements. Sometimes the pictorial elements consisted of clowns, seals and objects balanced on the end of noses, feet etc. and underlined this formal preoccupation. The tension and general idea of 'look at me' together with the showbiz aspect of the circus contributed to the presentation and selling of merchandise.

Lester Bookbinder/Federico advertisement, 1A Wyner, 1957.

Paul Rand, 1944.

Balloon. A compelling symbol because of its tension and airborne aspiration. Sexual overtones. One of the many objects of childhood associated with pleasurable memories. These memories are again invoked when applied to adult interests and products. Various characteristics of the balloon may be alluded to for instance; inflation, lightness, etc.

Airfilled and therefore 'indigestion' is the characteristic referred to. Headline says, 'Upset stomach – when you feel ready to burst', Parke Davis, Mendell/Oberer. Germany, 1968.

Magazine cover, 1955. Designer Henry Wolf. Photographer Dan Wynn, USA.
Balloon (Speech). Derives from the language of comic books. Totally absorbed in to the common currency of communication.

Trade advertisement, CBS Radio Network, 1958. Lou Dorfsman, USA

Catalogue cover for type material. Harris-Intertype 1970. Nohl/Hauer/Soderman.

Ballot Box. Useful symbol for elections or the concept of democracy. Not much use outside of its prime meaning.
Banana. The ultimate phallic symbol. The verbal expression 'banana-skin humour' derives from the comic book where characters slip on the discarded item. A basic humourous situation.
Banner. The diagonal strip (usually red) on the corner of magazines and other graphic media. Unsophisticated in origin but has a great sense of urgency. The message at an angle of 45 degrees was a dynamic learnt from the Bauhaus and reached epidemic proportions in 30's and 40's. An indispensable device which defies parody.
Bar Diagram. (Histogram). Comparative device. More useful than the 'cake' when the tolerances are finer. (See Diagrams and Bottle tops).
Barbed Wire. Extremely tactile image. Its war associations are often referred to. Sometimes more imaginatively it is used to evoke (by juxtaposition) the opposite quality of 'fragility'.

Record cover 'Persecution & Mass murder'. Falk / Bergentz / Lenskog, 1966. Unequivocal visual message. (See Star).

Magazine cover 'Direction', Paul Rand 1940. Ironic Christmas parcel.

Barometer. Like the thermometer, a powerful image. Used in relation to its prime meaning (weather). It is also used to convey the general concept of 'measuring pressure' or simply 'measuring'. (See calibrations). Sometimes used as an analogy for hierarchies in the social or business fields. The word 'barometer' has associations with measuring opinion.
Basket. Powerful graphic shape. Usually the meaning is closely associated with its prime function. For instance, the idea of 'rejection' with a waste-paper basket or 'consumer spending' with shopping and supermarket baskets.

Advertisement for typefounders Alfieri & Lacroix, 1955. Franco Grignani, Italy. The copy begins, 'Bad printed matter is invariably doomed'. The typography echoes the lines of movement derived from comic books.
Bee. An insect regarded with some affection. A traditional symbol of industry. It appears on many coats of arms of towns. Sometimes oblique reference is made to it as a 'lover' symbol (birds and bees). Being a social animal it is naturally connected with the idea of socialisation.
Beehive. Easily formalised as a series of circles or hexagons. The symbolism is usually that of 'Industry' or 'socialisation'. Christian emblem for the Church, the bees represent the 'faithful'.

Direct mail for Jack Wolfgang Beck, 1957. Jack Wolfgang Beck, USA. The copy reads 'design/industry'. A visual metaphor.
Before and After. A basic cliché of folk and popular advertising, usually associated with quick medicinal cures. The basic idea was given a 'facelift' in the sixties.

The Dictionary of Visual Clichés made readers aware of visual metaphors and the symbolic meaning behind them, and provided examples of how designers have turned these clichés into a shorthand visual language that communicates complex ideas.

Bow and Arrow

Bow and Arrow. The bow and arrow complement each other. Traditional symbol of the hunt. Apollo, Diana and Eros among other gods and godesses are represented with bows and arrows. Strongest association today is with Eros and his 'human targets' of love.

Zodiacal sign of Saggitarius the archer.
1st anti-aircraft command flash, 1943.
Bow and arrow to symbolise concept of penetration into countryside. Hans Schleger, UK.

Bowler Hat. Sometimes a symbol for England or Great Britain, particularly in the fiscal or business area. It sometimes has a more general connotation of bureaucracy.

Box. Fundamental graphic device with strong psychological overtones (as in Pandora's box). There is usually a relationship between the basic graphic devices and the multiplicity of word couplings and figures of speech that associate with the word. For instance: Box-office, box-room, shooting box, theatre box, box clever, box pleat, etc. (See also Heart, House, Wheel).

Brain. The characteristic side elevation popular as a symbol for whatever part of the brain is referred to: memory, reasoning, imagination, 'brain-washing' etc. (See Cranium).

Branch. Well used in its diagramatic application (see Diagram) as in railway maps. In its naturalistic form (tree) was part of an early (thirties and forties) repertoire of organic forms which were invested with symbolic meaning. The animal, mineral and vegetable kingdom was the richest source of symbolism from pre-history to the present century, although some artifacts were invested with symbolic significance. In this century the repertoire of symbols has enlarged to include the artifacts of our industrial culture.
The concept of the tree of life is fundamental. In folklore and diverse religions, gods and spirits inhabited trees as did many Christian saints. We speak of having a family tree. The branch is thus a natural symbol for growth.

Branding Marks. Part of the repertoire of House and Holding marks by which the movable property and livestock of farmers etc is distinguished.

Credit titles for the cowboy film by Saul Bass. These consisted of cattle brand marks.

Breasts. The life-giving milk of the human breast is one of the principal themes in the representation of woman in art from the caveman onwards.
The concept of the eternal mother figure is conspicuous in pagan and Christian cultures from the Egyptian goddess Anouke to the Madonna and Child.
The interest in the breast in our own time is largely erotic or aesthetic. The gratuitous representation of breasts to sell ideas and products unrelated to their prime significance (bra manufacturers excepted) is a contemporary phenomenon.
Like other fundamental and profound objects such as the box, the sun and moon, they are easily represented in graphic terms.

Robert Brownjohn. Poster for Robert Fraser Gallery. The obsession is made flesh.

Andre Francois. Cover for Gilbey Wines.

Bricks

Andre Francois. Cover for SIA Journal. A 'reductio ad absurdum' reminds us of the breasts' function.

Bricks. Popular as a symbol for primary education. A fifties cliche for 'simplicity' (literally, it's child's play). Sometimes a symbol for the 'elementary facts'. Naturally used by the building trade but also by investment and money lending firms (building for the future etc).

Direct mail for Herman Miller Furniture Co., 1955. George Tscherny, USA. 'ABC of modern furniture' runs the copy. A universal symbol of simplicity combines with comprehensiveness.

Annual Report cover, Uris Buildings Corporation, 1962. George Tscherny, USA. Children's building bricks as a substitute for the real thing.

Britannia. A symbol for Great Britain usually as a basis for parody.

Brush

Brush. Traditional symbol for 'Art'. A simple visual version of the literary figure of speech 'metonomy', where the whole activity is summed up by the part; as in a man of the cloth, forsook the plough for the sword, etc.

Poster, Los Angeles County Museum of Art. Exhibition of American Paintings, 1966. Louis Danziger, USA. Fusion of brush (condensing of Art) with flag (America).

Book jacket, Paul Theobald, 1946. 'Modern Art in Advertising'. Paul Rand, USA. An early use of substitution (metonomy) of brush (part) for Art (whole).

Poster, Museum of Modern Art, 1941. For exhibition of American painting. Paul Rand, USA. Multiple fusion of visual puns (brush/beard) with symbolic hat (American flag/Uncle Sam).

Building. The portrayal of a specific building to symbolise specific places, activities or ideas. Big Ben symbolises London for instance. Le Moulin Rouge symbolises a whole epoch.

Poster for Advise and Consent. Saul Bass, USA.

Illustration for an article on prohibition in America, 1956. Mark Boxer, UK.
The idea of 'taking the lid off' domed buildings is an obsessive one. Sometimes it has a connotation of 'exposure'. The choice of building in both examples is symbolic of justice.

Bulb. A light bulb is a symbol for an idea or creativity. There may be some association with the idea of 'Divine light' i.e. inspiration.

Self promotion 'creative' advertisers 1958 Calkins & Holden USA

Bull. Symbol of strength and fertility. Associated with kingship in ancient Egypt. To some extent it still symbolises authority and power among the farming community. It is used (by association) by heavy industry, such as construction companies, as a symbol of strength and reliability.

Bulldog. A relatively recent symbol for Great Britain.

Bullet Holes

Bullet. As the nature of communication is basically aggressive, the use of a bullet as a visual symbol is compulsive even when the context is not warlike.

John F. Kennedy
Medgar Evers
Martin Luther King, Jr
Robert F. Kennedy
NEXT?

Political advertisement. Chuck Strausser, USA. The image is a literal parallel to the bitter copy, 'write to your senator or congressman while you still have one'.

Advertisement for lipstick. Yardley & Company Ltd, UK. Design by Angela Landels/John Castle, Art director David Cooper. The copy uses phrases like 'A woman's ammunition' and 'sure-fire lipsticks' which underline the aggressive and hunting nature of courtship and sexual attraction. The lipstick and bullet is a visual pun.

Bullet Holes. When the subject matter is appropriate, a spray of bullet holes is a convenient graphic device by virtue of its elementary form and the possibility of its random disposition. The popular market sometimes demands frayed edges and in extreme cases real holes.

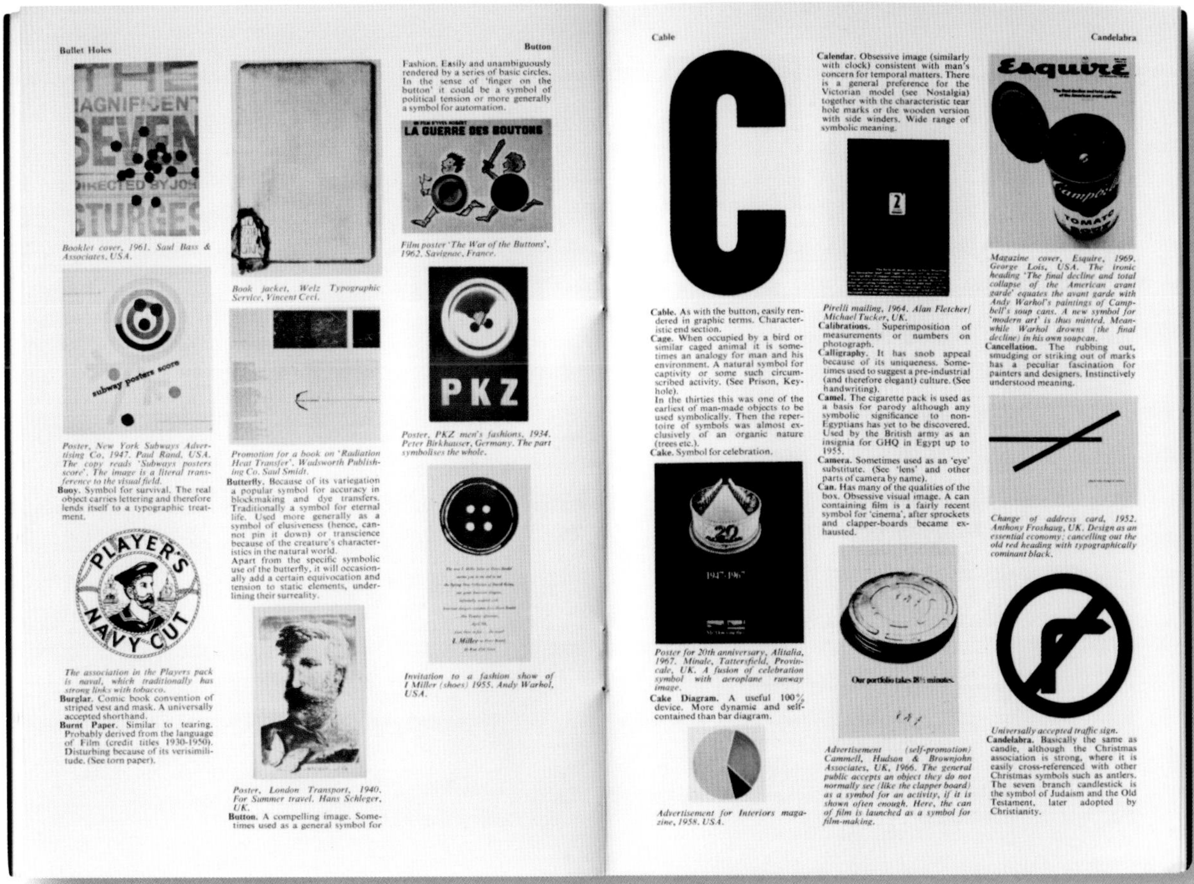
Bullet Holes

Booklet cover, 1961. Saul Bass & Associates, USA.

Poster, New York Subways Advertising Co, 1947. Paul Rand, USA. The copy reads 'Subways posters score'. The image is a literal transference to the visual field.

Buoy. Symbol for survival. The real object carries lettering and therefore lends itself to a typographic treatment.

The association in the Players pack is naval, which traditionally has strong links with tobacco.

Burglar. Comic book convention of striped vest and mask. A universally accepted shorthand.

Burnt Paper. Similar to tearing. Probably derived from the language of Film (credit titles 1930-1950). Disturbing because of its verisimilitude. (See torn paper).

Book jacket, Welz Typographic Service, Vincent Ceci.

Promotion for a book on 'Radiation Heat Transfer'. Wadsworth Publishing Co. Saul Smidt.

Butterfly. Because of its variegation a popular symbol for accuracy in blockmaking and dye transfers. Traditionally a symbol for eternal life. Used more generally as a symbol of elusiveness (hence, cannot pin it down) or transcience because of the creature's characteristics in the natural world.
Apart from the specific symbolic use of the butterfly, it will occasionally add a certain equivocation and tension to static elements, underlining their surreality.

Poster, London Transport, 1940. For Summer travel. Hans Schleger, UK.

Button. A compelling image. Sometimes used as a general symbol for

Button

Fashion. Easily and unambiguously rendered by a series of basic circles. In the sense of 'finger on the button' it could be a symbol of political tension or more generally a symbol for automation.

Film poster 'The War of the Buttons', 1962. Savignac, France.

Poster, PKZ men's fashions, 1934. Peter Birkhauser, Germany. The part symbolises the whole.

Invitation to a fashion show of I Miller (shoes) 1955. Andy Warhol, USA.

Cable

Cable. As with the button, easily rendered in graphic terms. Characteristic end section.

Cage. When occupied by a bird or similar caged animal it is sometimes an analogy for man and his environment. A natural symbol for captivity or some such circumscribed activity. (See Prison, Keyhole).
In the thirties this was one of the earliest of man-made objects to be used symbolically. Then the repertoire of symbols was almost exclusively of an organic nature (trees etc.).

Cake. Symbol for celebration.

Poster for 20th anniversary, Alitalia, 1967. Minale, Tattersfield, Provincale, UK. A fusion of celebration symbol with aeroplane runway image.

Cake Diagram. A useful 100% device. More dynamic and self-contained than bar diagram.

Advertisement for Interiors magazine, 1958. USA.

Calendar. Obsessive image (similarly with clock) consistent with man's concern for temporal matters. There is a general preference for the Victorian model (see Nostalgia) together with the characteristic tear hole marks or the wooden version with side winders. Wide range of symbolic meaning.

Pirelli mailing, 1964. Alan Fletcher/Michael Tucker, UK.

Calibrations. Superimposition of measurements or numbers on photograph.

Calligraphy. It has snob appeal because of its uniqueness. Sometimes used to suggest a pre-industrial (and therefore elegant) culture. (See handwriting).

Camel. The cigarette pack is used as a basis for parody although any symbolic significance to non-Egyptians has yet to be discovered. Used by the British army as an insignia for GHQ in Egypt up to 1955.

Camera. Sometimes used as an 'eye' substitute. (See 'lens' and other parts of camera by name).

Can. Has many of the qualities of the box. Obsessive visual image. A can containing film is a fairly recent symbol for 'cinema', after sprockets and clapper-boards became exhausted.

Advertisement (self-promotion) Cammell, Hudson & Brownjohn Associates, UK, 1966. The general public accepts an object they do not normally see (like the clapper board) as a symbol for an activity, if it is shown often enough. Here, the can of film is launched as a symbol for film-making.

Candelabra

Magazine cover, Esquire, 1969. George Lois, USA. The ironic heading 'The final decline and total collapse of the American avant garde' equates the avant garde with Andy Warhol's paintings of Campbell's soup cans. A new symbol for 'modern art' is thus minted. Meanwhile Warhol drowns (the final decline) in his own soupcan.

Cancellation. The rubbing out, smudging or striking out of marks has a peculiar fascination for painters and designers. Instinctively understood meaning.

Change of address card, 1952. Anthony Froshaug, UK. Design as an essential economy; cancelling out the old red heading with typographically cominant black.

Universally accepted traffic sign.

Candelabra. Basically the same as candle, although the Christmas association is strong, where it is easily cross-referenced with other Christmas symbols such as antlers. The seven branch candlestick is the symbol of Judaism and the Old Testament, later adopted by Christianity.

No. 17: **The Many Faces of Mao**

Back Story

While partner Kit Hinrichs was teaching a design class at the California College of Arts and Crafts in San Francisco, a student named Jenny Wong told him she was going to Shanghai to visit her parents and asked if she could bring him a souvenir. "Maybe a Mao button," he said. To his surprise, Jenny returned with a hand-crafted bamboo case filled with Mao buttons made by her father, Xue-shi Shen, a designer of Mao buttons during the Cultural Revolution. For nearly a year, Shen had been held under "house arrest" in the button factory after officials accused him of desecrating Mao's image by leaving a paintbrush on a button. Jenny's gift prompted partner Linda Hinrichs to challenge her brother, Dr. Larry Davis, and his two kids to find more buttons while on his 1988 medical sabbatical to Shanghai. They returned with so many Mao objects that Linda turned them into a Pentagram Paper.

During China's Cultural Revolution (1966–76), Chairman Mao Zedong attained a godlike stature that saw his portrait displayed on billboards, posters, statues, busts, in homes at the family altar, and on buttons that followers pinned to their jackets. A daily ritual for the masses was bowing three times before Chairman Mao's portrait or bust, singing the national anthem, reading passages from Mao's *The Little Red Book*, and wishing him "ten thousand years." More than a fad, the Mao buttons were a show of patriotic fervor and an ever-present reminder of living the ideals of the Cultural Revolution. When the Mao cult was at its peak around 1967, factories in Beijing, Shanghai, and Canton (Guangzhou) turned out more than six million Chairman Mao buttons a month in about twenty different variations. Desecration of Mao's likeness was viewed as cause for imprisonment. By the early 1970s, the extreme aspects of Mao as a divine presence were discouraged, and Mao buttons disappeared from public view.

Two years ago Jenny Wong, a student in Kit Hinrichs'
design class at the California College of Arts and Crafts,
asked if she could bring him a souvenir from Shanghai,
where she grew up and her parents still lived. "A Mao button
or Red star," Kit requested. To his surprise, Jenny
returned with a hand-crafted wooden case filled with buttons.
What she hadn't revealed to him before she left
was that her father, Xue-shi Shen, was an artist/craftsman
who designed Mao buttons during the years of the
Cultural Revolution. This remarkable gift led to a challenge
to Linda Hinrichs' brother, Dr. Larry Davis, to
seek out more Mao buttons on his 1988 medical sabbatical
to Shanghai. At first, Larry and his two teenage
children found none, but as they became more adventurous,
they discovered numerous button sources, eventually
amassing an incredible collection of their own. Pentagram
staffers Shirley Yee and Albert Tong further
augmented this collection on their visits to China with their
parents. Astonishingly, out of the dozens of Mao
buttons collected, only one was a duplicate. Current politics
aside, this amazing set of icons represents a curious
and special part of 20th-century history.

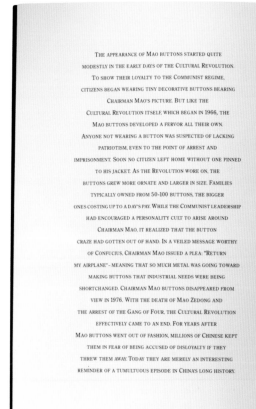

THE APPEARANCE OF MAO BUTTONS STARTED QUITE
MODESTLY IN THE EARLY DAYS OF THE CULTURAL REVOLUTION.
TO SHOW THEIR LOYALTY TO THE COMMUNIST REGIME,
CITIZENS BEGAN WEARING TINY DECORATIVE BUTTONS BEARING
CHAIRMAN MAO'S PICTURE. BUT LIKE THE
CULTURAL REVOLUTION ITSELF, WHICH BEGAN IN 1966, THE
MAO BUTTONS DEVELOPED A FERVOR ALL THEIR OWN.
ANYONE NOT WEARING A BUTTON WAS SUSPECTED OF LACKING
PATRIOTISM, EVEN TO THE POINT OF ARREST AND
IMPRISONMENT. SOON NO CITIZEN LEFT HOME WITHOUT ONE PINNED
TO HIS JACKET. AS THE REVOLUTION WORE ON, THE
BUTTONS GREW MORE ORNATE AND LARGER IN SIZE. FAMILIES
TYPICALLY OWNED FROM 50-100 BUTTONS, THE BIGGER
ONES COSTING UP TO A DAY'S PAY. WHILE THE COMMUNIST LEADERSHIP
HAD ENCOURAGED A PERSONALITY CULT TO ARISE AROUND
CHAIRMAN MAO, IT REALIZED THAT THE BUTTON
CRAZE HAD GOTTEN OUT OF HAND. IN A VEILED MESSAGE WORTHY
OF CONFUCIUS, CHAIRMAN MAO ISSUED A PLEA: "RETURN
MY AIRPLANE" - MEANING THAT SO MUCH METAL WAS GOING TOWARD
MAKING BUTTONS THAT INDUSTRIAL NEEDS WERE BEING
SHORTCHANGED. CHAIRMAN MAO BUTTONS DISAPPEARED FROM
VIEW IN 1976. WITH THE DEATH OF MAO ZEDONG AND
THE ARREST OF THE GANG OF FOUR, THE CULTURAL REVOLUTION
EFFECTIVELY CAME TO AN END. FOR YEARS AFTER
MAO BUTTONS WENT OUT OF FASHION, MILLIONS OF CHINESE KEPT
THEM IN FEAR OF BEING ACCUSED OF DISLOYALTY IF THEY
THREW THEM AWAY. TODAY THEY ARE MERELY AN INTERESTING
REMINDER OF A TUMULTUOUS EPISODE IN CHINA'S LONG HISTORY.

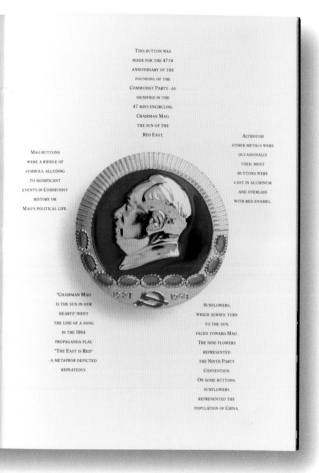

THIS BUTTON WAS
MADE FOR THE 47TH
ANNIVERSARY OF THE
FOUNDING OF THE
COMMUNIST PARTY - AS
SIGNIFIED IN THE
47 RAYS ENCIRCLING
CHAIRMAN MAO,
THE SUN OF THE
RED EAST

ALTHOUGH
OTHER METALS WERE
OCCASIONALLY
USED, MOST
BUTTONS WERE
CAST IN ALUMINUM
AND OVERLAID
WITH RED ENAMEL.

MAO BUTTONS
WERE A RIDDLE OF
SYMBOLS, ALLUDING
TO SIGNIFICANT
EVENTS IN COMMUNIST
HISTORY OR
MAO'S POLITICAL LIFE.

"CHAIRMAN MAO
IS THE SUN IN OUR
HEARTS" WENT
THE LINE OF A SONG
IN THE 1964
PROPAGANDA PLAY,
"THE EAST IS RED"
- A METAPHOR DEPICTED
REPEATEDLY.

SUNFLOWERS,
WHICH ALWAYS TURN
TO THE SUN,
FACED TOWARD MAO.
THE NINE FLOWERS
REPRESENTED
THE NINTH PARTY
CONVENTION.
ON SOME BUTTONS,
SUNFLOWERS
REPRESENTED THE
POPULATION OF CHINA.

Research for this Pentagram Paper was greatly advanced when Xue-shi Shen, a Mao button artisan, came to San Francisco to visit his daughter, Jenny. The wooden box, top left, and buttons, bottom right, were all designed by Shen.

WHILE MOST BUTTON PROFILES OF
CHAIRMAN MAO DEPICT HIM FACING LEFT,
THE REASON HAD LITTLE TO DO WITH
POLITICAL BIAS. IT JUST HAPPENED THAT
THE PHOTOGRAPH FROM WHICH
THE AUTHORIZED MASTER CAST WAS MADE
SHOWED HIM FACING IN THAT DIRECTION.

TOTALITARIAN
SOCIETIES FREQUENTLY
SUCCUMB TO
PERSONALITY CULTS. IN
RECENT MEMORY,
STALIN, LENIN, HITLER,
KHOMEINI ALL
COMMANDED A FANATICAL
FOLLOWING, TO THE
POINT WHERE IDEOLOGY
AND LEADER WERE
VIEWED AS ONE. FOR
DECADES, MAO ZEDONG
PERSONIFIED CHINESE
COMMUNISM. MAO'S
ASCENT BEGAN IN
1934 WHEN HE LED THE
RED ARMY ON A

6000-MILE LONG MARCH
ACROSS CHINA TO
ESCAPE NATIONALIST
FORCES. IN 1949
WHEN THE COMMUNIST
PARTY GAINED
POWER IN CHINA, MAO
WAS SEEN AS THE
LIBERATOR OF THE MASSES.
BUT AS HIS GREAT
LEAP FORWARD ECONOMIC
POLICIES FAILED TO
LIFT CHINA FROM POVERTY
AND BACKWARDNESS,
MAO SECURED HIS
POSITION BY ELEVATING
HIMSELF ABOVE POLITICS
TO THE STATURE OF
A DEMIGOD.

MAO'S PROGRAM TO "REHABILITATE"
THE INTELLECTUAL CLASS THROUGH FARM
LABOR WAS IDEALIZED IN IMAGES
OF HIMSELF IN PEASANT CLOTHES. MAO'S
HARSH POLICIES BEGAN TO SHIFT
IN THE EARLY 1970S WHEN HE
ESTABLISHED LIMITED DIPLOMATIC
RELATIONS WITH THE WEST. A SYMBOLIC
GESTURE WAS THE EXCHANGE OF
PING-PONG TEAMS WITH AMERICA, THEN
DUBBED "PING-PONG DIPLOMACY."

ARTISANS ALL OVER CHINA
WERE ENLISTED TO DESIGN
PATRIOTIC BUTTONS BEARING THE
IMAGE OF MAO ZEDONG.
THE MASTER CASTS OF MAO'S
FACE WERE PURCHASED
FROM A CENTRAL SOURCE. THE
SIZE, SHAPE, DECORATIVE BORDER
AND SYMBOLIC IMAGERY OF
EACH BUTTON WERE LEFT TO THE
CREATIVE DISCRETION OF
INDIVIDUAL BUTTON DESIGNERS.

The cult of Mao generated thousands of Mao likenesses in various materials. Buttons grew so large that Mao himself asked citizens to stop because the aluminum used to make them was creating a shortage in plane manufacturing.

CHAIRMAN MAO BUTTONS RANGED IN SIZE
FROM DISCREET 1/4-INCH PINS TO 6-INCH
DIAMETER BADGES. TYPICALLY THE SMALLER
ONES WERE PRODUCED DURING THE EARLY
YEARS OF THE CULTURAL REVOLUTION.
AS SUSPICION AND FEAR OVERPOWERED REASON
IN THE LATTER YEARS OF WHAT HAS BECOME

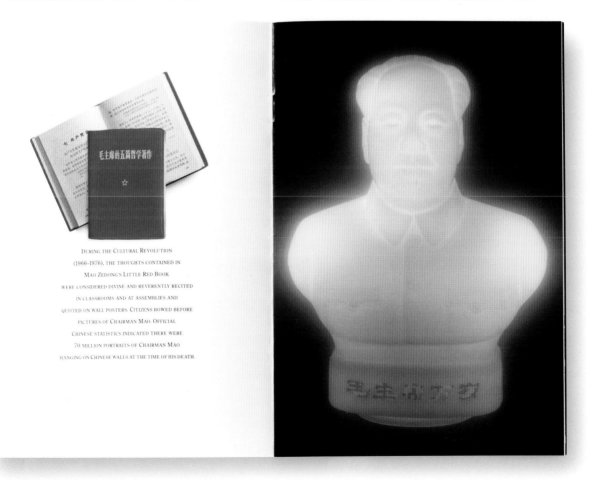

KNOWN IN CHINA AS THE "TEN YEARS'
TURMOIL," MAO BUTTONS GREW TO THE SIZE
OF DISKS. THE LARGE MEDALLION BUTTONS
WERE TIED TO A RIBBON AND WORN AROUND
THE NECK. THE SIZE AND SHAPE OF
BUTTONS WERE ALSO DICTATED BY FASHION;
WHEN BIG WAS "IN," HUGE IMAGES OF
MAO WERE EVIDENT EVERYWHERE.

DURING THE CULTURAL REVOLUTION
(1966-1976), THE THOUGHTS CONTAINED IN
MAO ZEDONG'S LITTLE RED BOOK
WERE CONSIDERED DIVINE AND REVERENTLY RECITED
IN CLASSROOMS AND AT ASSEMBLIES AND
QUOTED ON WALL POSTERS. CITIZENS BOWED BEFORE
PICTURES OF CHAIRMAN MAO. OFFICIAL
CHINESE STATISTICS INDICATED THERE WERE
70 MILLION PORTRAITS OF CHAIRMAN MAO
HANGING ON CHINESE WALLS AT THE TIME OF HIS DEATH.

No. 23: **Cigar Papers**

Before they are smoked, Havana cigars reveal their spirit, provenance, and quality through an esoteric ritual of banding, wrapping, boxing, and marking. Hence, the word *vitola*, a term that embodies the classification of the size, shape, and form of individual cigars, is often used interchangeably with the identifying labels themselves. Like all good packaging, the best cigar label designs communicate the quality and refinement of the product. It is said that the first *vitolas* were produced by Anton Bock at his factory, El Aguila de Oro, soon after 1845, when Ramon Allones, proprietor of the Havana factory La Eminencia, began to pack his cigars in cedar boxes decorated inside and out with printed labels. Lithography had arrived in Cuba in the early 1800s, and the Havana cigar and printing industries developed hand in hand. Financial incentives offered by wealthy cigar factory owners and opportunities to do exquisite work lured many famous lithographers to Cuba. This led in 1907 to the founding of the Compañia Litográfica de la Habana for the production of cigar labels in fine relief, glowing with vivid color and gold leaf.

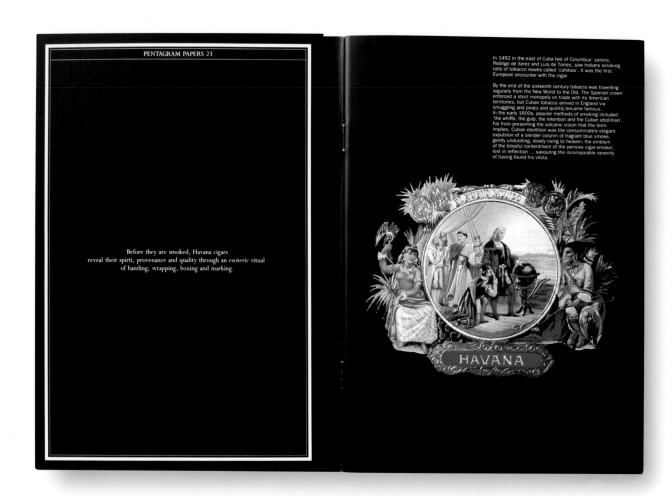

Before they are smoked, Havana cigars
reveal their spirit, provenance and quality through an esoteric ritual
of banding, wrapping, boxing and marking.

In 1492 in the east of Cuba two of Columbus' sailors, Rodrigo de Xerez and Luis de Torres, saw Indians smoking rolls of tobacco leaves called 'cohibas'. It was the first European encounter with the cigar.

By the end of the sixteenth century tobacco was travelling regularly from the New World to the Old. The Spanish crown enforced a strict monopoly on trade with its American territories, but Cuban tobacco arrived in England via smuggling and piracy and quickly became famous.
In the early 1600s, popular methods of smoking included 'the whiffe, the gulp, the retention and the Cuban ebollition'. Far from presenting the volcanic vision that the term implies, Cuban ebollition was the consummately elegant expulsion of a slender column of fragrant blue smoke, gently undulating, slowly rising to heaven; the emblem of the blissful contentment of the pensive cigar-smoker, lost in reflection … savouring the incomparable serenity of having found his vitola.

HAVANA

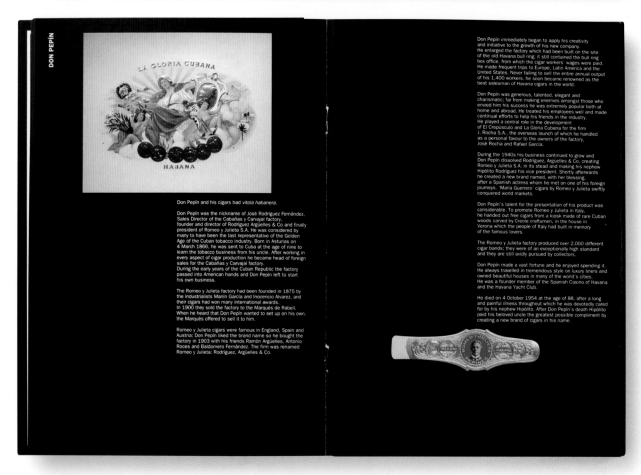

DON PEPIN

Don Pepín and his cigars had *vitola habanera*.

Don Pepín was the nickname of José Rodríguez Fernández, Sales Director of the Cabañas y Carvajal factory, founder and director of Rodríguez Argüelles & Co and finally president of Romeo y Julieta S.A. He was considered by many to have been the last representative of the Golden Age of the Cuban tobacco industry. Born in Asturias on 4 March 1866, he was sent to Cuba at the age of nine to learn the tobacco business from his uncle. After working in every aspect of cigar production he became head of foreign sales for the Cabañas y Carvajal factory.
During the early years of the Cuban Republic the factory passed into American hands and Don Pepín left to start his own business.

The Romeo y Julieta factory had been founded in 1875 by the industrialists Marín García and Inocencio Alvarez, and their cigars had won many international awards.
In 1900 they sold the factory to the Marqués de Rabell. When he heard that Don Pepín wanted to set up on his own, the Marqués offered to sell it to him.

Romeo y Julieta cigars were famous in England, Spain and Austria; Don Pepín liked the brand name so he bought the factory in 1903 with his friends Ramón Argüelles, Antonio Roces and Baldomero Fernández. The firm was renamed Romeo y Julieta: Rodríguez, Argüelles & Co.

Don Pepín immediately began to apply his creativity and initiative to the growth of his new company.
He enlarged the factory which had been built on the site of the old Havana bull ring; it still contained the bull ring box office, from which the cigar workers' wages were paid. He made frequent trips to Europe, Latin America and the United States. Never failing to sell the entire annual output of his 1,400 workers, he soon became renowned as the best salesman of Havana cigars in the world.

Don Pepín was generous, talented, elegant and charismatic; far from making enemies amongst those who envied him his success he was extremely popular both at home and abroad. He treated his employees well and made continual efforts to help his friends in the industry.
He played a central role in the development of El Crepúsculo and La Gloria Cubana for the firm J. Rocha S.A., the overseas launch of which he handled as a personal favour to the owners of the factory, José Rocha and Rafael García.

During the 1940s his business continued to grow and Don Pepín dissolved Rodríguez, Argüelles & Co. creating Romeo y Julieta S.A. in its stead and making his nephew Hipólito Rodríguez his vice president. Shortly afterwards he created a new brand named, with her blessing, after a Spanish actress whom he met on one of his foreign journeys. 'María Guerrero' cigars by Romeo y Julieta swiftly conquered world markets.

Don Pepín's talent for the presentation of his product was considerable. To promote Romeo y Julieta in Italy, he handed out free cigars from a kiosk made of rare Cuban woods carved by Creole craftsmen, in the house in Verona which the people of Italy had built in memory of the famous lovers.

The Romeo y Julieta factory produced over 2,000 different cigar bands; they were of an exceptionally high standard and they are still avidly pursued by collectors.

Don Pepín made a vast fortune and he enjoyed spending it. He always travelled in tremendous style on luxury liners and owned beautiful houses in many of the world's cities. He was a founder member of the Spanish Casino of Havana and the Havana Yacht Club.

He died on 4 October 1954 at the age of 88, after a long and painful illness throughout which he was devotedly cared for by his nephew Hipólito. After Don Pepín's death Hipólito paid his beloved uncle the greatest possible compliment by creating a new brand of cigars in his name.

Cuban cigar makers have designed commemorative bands to mark historic events and to honor politicians and military heroes. Custom labels have also been produced for commercial interests including Shell Oil, Sloppy Joe's Bar, and Pirelli Tires.

A souvenir from H Upmann of the foundation in September 1955 of the Cuban Association of Vitolfilia (AVC).

Vitola produced by Rodríguez Argüelles & Co (Romeo y Julieta) to commemorate the end of World War I.

Two Men - Two Nations. Vitola produced by Punch to commemorate a visit made to the President of Brazil, Getulio Vargas, by Teddy Roosevelt.

Vitola from Por Larrañaga produced as a "souvenir of the wedding of Ignacio and Maritere, 14 October 1956, Havana."

Vitolas produced in 1952 for the Fiftieth Anniversary of Cuban Independence.

José Julián Marti Pérez was born in Havana on 28 January 1853 and spent his life writing poetry and prose calling for Cuba's independence from Spain. He was exiled in 1871 but in 1895 he returned to Cuba to fight for his beliefs. On 19 May of that year he was killed at the age of 42 in a battle at Dos Rios. On the eve of his death he wrote to a friend: 'Every day I am in danger of giving my life for my country and my duty'.

The mulatto general Antonio Maceo Grajales, 'The Bronze Titan', was born on 14 June 1848. He enlisted in the revolutionary army as a private soldier on 12 October 1868 and displayed such valour that day that he was immediately made a sergeant. He fought bravely throughout the war (1868-1878), rising through the ranks to become a major general. When Spain proposed a general amnesty in return for the surrender of the rebels only Maceo believed that the struggle could still be won, as he stated in his famous 'Protest of Baragua'. However he could not hold out alone and went into exile in Jamaica. He returned to Cuba in 1895 and fought a brilliant campaign of battles throughout the length of the island. He was killed the following year.

Máximo Gómez Baéz was born in what is now the Dominican Republic on 18 November 1836. He came to Cuba to farm but at the outbreak of the Ten Years' War of Independence he joined the rebel forces as a general. He proved himself a superb military strategist and personally led the first cavalry charge of the Cuban troops. At the end of the Ten Years' War he left Cuba but returned with José Marti in 1895. Unlike Marti he survived the war and became a Cuban citizen. He died in Havana on 17 June 1905.

Vitolas from the Partagas factory. Fidel Castro Ruz, Camilo Cienfuegos Gorriarán and Ernesto 'Che' Guevara de la Serna were the three commanders of the Cuban Revolution.

Camilo was handsome, charismatic and popular with everyone. He disappeared whilst on a solo flight from Camagüey to Havana in October 1959; it is supposed that his plane crashed into the sea.

Fidel Castro, who began the Revolution as a 26 year old lawyer in 1953, is President of the Republic of Cuba. His motives, personality and track record are the subjects of constant international controversy.

Ernesto 'Che' Guevara was an asthmatic Argentinian doctor who sailed with Fidel from Veracruz on 24 November 1956 to continue the Revolution. Guevara, 'The Soldier of the Americas', was killed in the Bolivian jungle on 8 October 1967.

Another 'solidarity' vitola, showing the symbol and colours of the 26 July Movement, was created to celebrate and commemorate Fidel's successful arrival in Havana after the long struggle to overthrow Batista.

From the factory of H. Upmann. There has been no official American Consul in Havana since 1961, when Eisenhower chose to take Fidel's demand that the American Embassy in Havana be reduced to eighteen diplomats as justification for breaking diplomatic ties. There were at that time eighteen Cuban diplomats in Washington and sixty American diplomats in Havana.

José Gener, owner of the brand Hoyo de Monterrey, sensibly produced a vitola which could continue to be used throughout the chaotic succession of presidents that governed Cuba during the first half of this century.

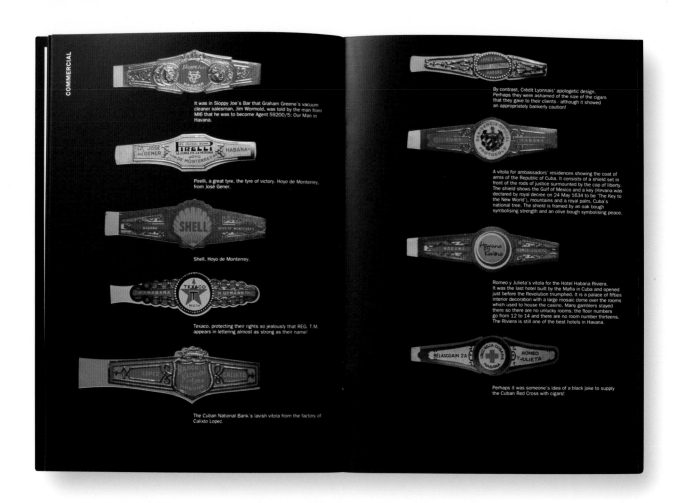

It was in Sloppy Joe's Bar that Graham Greene's vacuum cleaner salesman, Jim Wormold, was told by the man from MI6 that he was to become Agent 59200/5: Our Man in Havana.

Pirelli, a great tyre, the tyre of victory. Hoyo de Monterrey, from José Gener.

Shell, Hoyo de Monterrey.

Texaco, protecting their rights so jealously that REG. T.M. appears in lettering almost as strong as their name!

The Cuban National Bank's lavish vitola from the factory of Calixto López.

By contrast, Crédit Lyonnais' apologetic design. Perhaps they were ashamed of the size of the cigars that they gave to their clients - although it showed an appropriately bankerly caution!

A vitola for ambassadors' residences showing the coat of arms of the Republic of Cuba. It consists of a shield set in front of the rods of justice surmounted by the cap of liberty. The shield shows the Gulf of Mexico and a key (Havana was declared by royal decree on 24 May 1634 to be 'The Key to the New World'), mountains and a royal palm, Cuba's national tree. The shield is framed by an oak bough symbolising strength and an olive bough symbolising peace.

Romeo y Julieta's vitola for the Hotel Habana Riviera. It was the last hotel built by the Mafia in Cuba and opened just before the Revolution triumphed. It is a palace of fifties interior decoration with a large mosaic dome over the rooms which used to house the casino. Many gamblers stayed there so there are no unlucky rooms: the floor numbers go from 12 to 14 and there are no room number thirteens. The Riviera is still one of the best hotels in Havana.

Perhaps it was someone's idea of a black joke to supply the Cuban Red Cross with cigars!

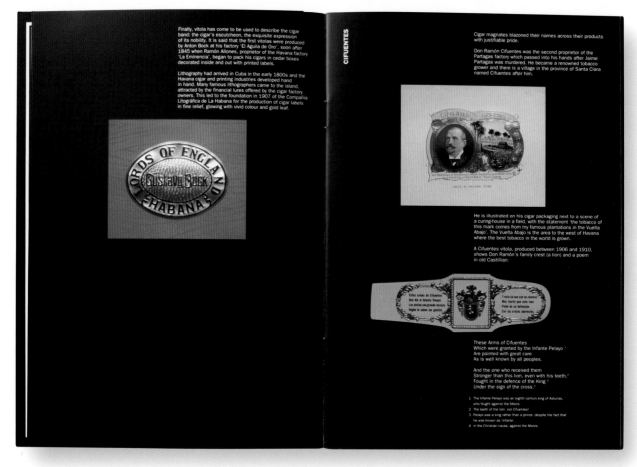

Finally, vitola has come to be used to describe the cigar band: the cigar's escutcheon, the exquisite expression of its nobility. It is said that the first vitolas were produced by Anton Bock at his factory 'El Aguila de Oro', soon after 1845 when Ramón Allones, proprietor of the Havana factory 'La Eminencia', began to pack his cigars in cedar boxes decorated inside and out with printed labels.

Lithography had arrived in Cuba in the early 1800s and the Havana cigar and printing industries developed hand in hand. Many famous lithographers came to the island, attracted by the financial lures offered by the cigar factory owners. This led to the foundation in 1907 of the Compañía Litográfica de La Habana for the production of cigar labels in fine relief, glowing with vivid colour and gold leaf.

Cigar magnates blazoned their names across their products with justifiable pride.

Don Ramón Cifuentes was the second proprietor of the Partagás factory which passed into his hands after Jaime Partagás was murdered. He became a renowned tobacco grower and there is a village in the province of Santa Clara named Cifuentes after him.

He is illustrated on his cigar packaging next to a scene of a curing-house in a field, with the statement 'the tobacco of this mark comes from my famous plantations in the Vuelta Abajo'. The Vuelta Abajo is the area to the west of Havana where the best tobacco in the world is grown.

A Cifuentes vitola, produced between 1906 and 1910, shows Don Ramón's family crest (a lion) and a poem in old Castilian:

These Arms of Cifuentes
Which were granted by the Infante Pelayo [1]
Are painted with great care
As is well known by all peoples.

And the one who received them
Stronger than this lion, even with his teeth,[2]
Fought in the defence of the King [3]
Under the sign of the cross.[4]

1 The Infante Pelayo was an eighth century king of Asturias, who fought against the Moors.
2 The teeth of the lion, not Cifuentes!
3 Pelayo was a king rather than a prince, despite the fact that he was known as 'Infante'.
4 In the Christian cause, against the Moors.

Tradition and provenance dictate the labeling and packaging of Cuban cigars, with gold foil and vivid colors used liberally to convey an air of nobility. The cedar box itself requires ten different labels, each with a special name and specific placement.

SON DE NEGROS EN CUBA

Cuando llegue la luna llena,
Iré a Santiago de Cuba,
Iré a Santiago
en un coche de aguas negras.
Iré a Santiago.
Cantarán los techos de palmera...
...Iré a Santiago.
Con la rubia cabeza de Fonseca.
Iré a Santiago.
Y con el rosal de Romeo y Julieta.
Iré a Santiago.
Mar de papel y plata de monedas.
Iré a Santiago.
¡Oh Cuba! ¡Oh ritmo de semillas secas!
Iré a Santiago.
¡Oh cintura caliente y gota de madera!
Iré a Santiago.
¡Arpa de troncos vivos, caimán, flor de tabaco!
Iré a Santiago.
Siempre dije que yo iría a Santiago
en un coche de agua negra...

SONG OF THE NEGROES OF CUBA

When the full moon rises,
I will go to Santiago de Cuba,
I will go to Santiago
In a coach of dark water.
I will go to Santiago.
The palm-thatched roofs will sing...
...I will go to Santiago.
With the blonde head of Fonseca.
I will go to Santiago.
With the roses of Romeo y Julieta.
I will go to Santiago.
Sea of paper and silver coins.
I will go to Santiago.
Oh Cuba! Oh rhythm of sapless seeds!
I will go to Santiago.
Oh warm waist and bead of wood!
I will go to Santiago.
Harp of live stalks, alligator, tobacco flower!
I will go to Santiago.
I always said I would go to Santiago
in a coach of dark water...

Federico García Lorca wove the roses in Capulet's garden and Fonseca's handsome face into a rhythmic chant based on old slave songs. * He likened the silver glitter of the sun on the Caribbean Sea to the medals on cigar packaging, and dedicated the poem to Fernando Ortiz.

* The structure of those songs has survived almost unchanged in Cuba. A single voice begins with a long 'calling' line, often improvised: 'Cuando llegue la luna llena, Iré a Santiago en un coche de aguas negras'. The other voices take their cue from the content and rhythm of that first line, and set up a throaty, percussive chant with which subsequent single voice lines are interspersed:

single voice: Con la rubia cabeza de Fonseca.
massed voices: Iré a Santiago.
single voice: Y con el rosal de Romeo y Julieta.
massed voices: Iré a Santiago.
single voice: Mar de papel y plata de monedas.
massed voices: Iré a Santiago.

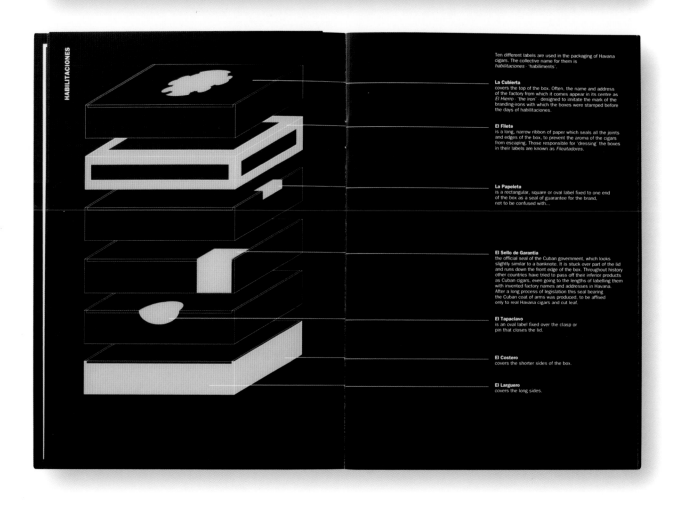

Ten different labels are used in the packaging of Havana cigars. The collective name for them is *habilitaciones* 'habiliments'.

La Cubierta
covers the top of the box. Often, the name and address of the factory from which it comes appear in its centre as *El Hierro* · 'the iron' · designed to imitate the mark of the branding-irons with which the boxes were stamped before the days of habilitaciones.

El Filete
is a long, narrow ribbon of paper which seals all the joints and edges of the box, to prevent the aroma of the cigars from escaping. Those responsible for 'dressing' the boxes in their labels are known as *Fileatadores*.

La Papeleta
is a rectangular, square or oval label fixed to one end of the box as a seal of guarantee for the brand, not to be confused with...

El Sello de Garantía
the official seal of the Cuban government, which looks slightly similar to a banknote. It is stuck over part of the lid and runs down the front edge of the box. Throughout history other countries have tried to pass off their inferior products as Cuban cigars, even going to the lengths of labelling them with invented factory names and addresses in Havana. After a long process of legislation this seal bearing the Cuban coat of arms was produced, to be affixed only to real Havana cigars and cut leaf.

El Tapaclavo
is an oval label fixed over the clasp or pin that closes the lid.

El Costero
covers the shorter sides of the box.

El Larguero
covers the long sides.

Personal Passions

Passion is the energy that springs from focusing on that which elicits excitement. It is the wellspring that nourishes the creative soul. Following one's personal passion is not always practical, expedient, or in vogue. Nor is it within one's control. It simply is. It is either nurtured and given free expression, or suppressed and rechanneled into forms that ultimately feel tentative, devoid of emotion, and lacking in vitality. Whether the passion is classical architecture, a fanciful little theater with watercolored sets, or a steadfast belief in the importance of the role of art in architecture, a conviction for the rightness of the direction comes through. Inherent in each is a single-minded clarity, freshness, and authenticity that reflects the courage of a passionate mind.

No. 7: **Ragazzini: Photographs of Bomarzo**

Bomarzo is a modest village sixty miles north of Rome, in wild, hilly country where the cardinals and Roman nobility hunted, built their villas, and entertained each other in the long, hot summers. When the lordship of the village passed to Pier Francesco Orsini in the sixteenth century, he created a remarkable garden, dedicated to his recently deceased wife, in the tangled woods below the old Orsini Castle. He filled it with astonishing sculptures, cut from the natural rock outcrops or from giant boulders that had fallen from the hills above.

In this rustic setting, sculptures emerge as if willed by nature from the undergrowth and shrubbery. Dragons, elephants, turtles, battling giants, and a miniature granite oak tree with an enormous granite acorn beside it populate the landscape. The sixteenth-century sculptor who carved them took as his inspiration the mythical characters in ancient fables.

Through the poetic lens of photographer Enzo Ragazzini, the Bomarzo sculptures take on an enchanted appearance. Weather-worn and moss-covered, they transport the viewer to a secret world where stone creatures rule the earth.

John McConnell designed this piece as a loose-sheet portfolio of photographic prints. The Bomarzo edition is the only Pentagram Paper produced this way. In retrospect, McConnell says, not binding the book was a mistake.

No. 20: **Architecture**

Back Story

In a used bookstore in Hastings, New York, partner Michael Bierut discovered an old pamphlet on architecture in a box filled with ephemera. He bought it, thinking it would make a nice welcome gift for architect James Biber, who had just become a partner of Pentagram. Written in 1926 by the renowned architectural critic Lewis Mumford, the pamphlet was part of a "Reading With a Purpose" educational series produced by the American Library Association of Chicago. Unlike Mumford's ambitious books, *Sticks and Stones*, *The Culture of Cities*, and *The City of History*, this essay was a short primer on architecture. It so cogently and simply explains the value of architecture that the Pentagram partners decided that new generations would find it of interest.

"Architecture is always having a conscious or an unconscious effect upon us. If we botch our buildings, crowd them together, or mistake their proper use, we cannot escape the results of our failure; if we plan them, order them, and design them with skill and love and sincerity, we shall, inevitably, participate in their triumph." So explained Lewis Mumford, the twentieth century's greatest American architectural critic, in a pamphlet on architecture written for the American Library Association of Chicago in 1926.

Taking issue with a popular notion that architecture is merely decoration, "like icing on a cake," Mumford explained that it encompassed a structure as stark as a corn elevator and as massively grand as an Egyptian tomb. "Architecture is not 'style' but building," he said.

"The forces that change architecture from one style to another are new materials, new modes of construction and the rise of new social habits, new modes of thinking; and the style of any period is the total result of these changes." Written for the layperson, Mumford's essay succinctly explains the impact of architecture on our lives and how it evolved over the ages.

Reading With a Purpose
=

ARCHITECTURE
By
LEWIS MUMFORD

CHICAGO
AMERICAN LIBRARY ASSOCIATION
1926

---

the same year published THE STORY OF UTOPIAS. *He is a lecturer on architecture in* American civilization *at the New School for Social Research, in New York.*

Whether the subject of Mr. Mumford's writing is architecture or industry, Chinese culture or the philosophy of Santayana, he never forgets its relation to human needs and values.

ARCHITECTURE

I

LESS than a century ago, John Ruskin set everyone thinking freshly about architecture. He discovered that buildings were alive; every stone had a tongue, and every tongue could tell a story. Many of us are still living by the enthusiasm that Ruskin awakened. We look forward to a trip to Europe which will permit us to read for ourselves these histories in stone—Westminster Abbey, Winchester Cathedral, the Belfrey of Bruges, Chartres, the remains of the Roman Colosseum, the great fragment of the Parthenon. Ruskin taught us to see beyond the mere "sight"; he showed that these buildings were the records of a community's life, its interests, its tastes, its economic organization, its social order, its religion.

But art did not "stop short with the cultivated court of the Empress Josephine." On the contrary, architecture is always with us, and a walk around the corner or across the fields will bring us face to face with it. What impression do the buildings that surround us make? Do they contribute, as Ruskin said architecture must, to our "mental health, power, and pleasure"? Or is this the sort of miracle that

9

Between 1925 and 1933, the American Library Association published an educational series of sixty-eight pamphlets on topics such as mental hygiene, sculpture, poetry, and psychology. Each was written by a noted authority.

plied it in various ways, using bricks, for example, as the mold and concrete in the core. Their bridges, roads, amphitheaters are still standing. It has the strength and simplicity of stone; it has the flexibility of brick; it has a massiveness of its own; and, in addition, since concrete can be poured into a mold, it makes possible fresh external shapes, which may fit the inside of the building as the glove fits the hand. Ferro-concrete, finally, need not be confined to flat surfaces and right angles. Erich Mendelsohn, the German architect, has shown how it can be modeled in the mass, as the sculptor models clay.

Wood gives still another type of construction. It leads to frame construction; for, like steel, a relatively light piece of wood will carry a heavy load when placed on end. Bind the frame together, form a box, fill the intervening space with bark, and you have the Long House of the Iroquois Indian; cover it with bamboo and thatch, and you have the simple Japanese dwelling; make the timber a little more solid, to stand up against heavy storms, and fill in the walls with clay or mud-and-twigs, or with flint, or with brick, and you have the half-timber house of medieval France, England, and Germany. Cover over a similar form with clapboards, and you have one of the early forms of the American house.

The habit of building frame houses in America made the transition to steel, for the framing of tall

buildings, fairly easy, except for architects who had been too thoroughly trained in the forms of pure masonry. In stone construction, each stone bears directly the load above it: take away a course of stones in the middle of the wall and the building topples. In frame construction, on the other hand, the load is distributed: no single part of the frame is essential, for the whole is knitted together: the wall ceases to be a support and becomes a curtain, and whereas a stone building could not possibly be lifted off its base and transported, it would be as easy to do this with a skyscraper as with a cottage, if we could have engines and rollers built on the same scale. Structurally, the building is complete when the frame has been put together. All other construction is merely to keep off the wind and the weather and to divide the interior space into suitable rooms.

Steel is an excellent material when height or a wide span is demanded. Its chief defects are that it rusts and conducts heat too easily; so it must be painted repeatedly to guard against the first danger, and, to prevent warping and buckling in a fire, it must be surrounded by a fire-proof, non-conducting material.

The dominance of steel in American urban architecture today is an exhibition of the way in which a technical achievement, the cheap manufacture of iron and structural steel, has worked hand in hand with a peculiar social situation—the concentration

past, he writes always with an eye pretty steadily fixed upon our own day, and our own country.

Of those who have treated architecture as a social art, I know no better modern exponent than Professor W. R. Lethaby. For him, architecture is not a matter of putting up a fine building, for show: it is rather the art of creating form in civilization, by giving to every house, street, neighborhood, landscape, factory, bridge, city, the imprint of a humane and excellent life. Although noted as an archeologist, Professor Lethaby has no desire to "restore the past." He stands for "free building," that is, the practice of building with respect to material, function, site, and human purpose, with the faith that if all these things are attended to intelligently with a loving eye, then "style" or "beauty" will come, too.

> FORM
> IN CIVILIZATION
> By W. R. Lethaby

> ARCHITECTURE
> AND DEMOCRACY
> By Claude Bragdon
>
> THE AUTOBIOGRAPHY
> OF AN IDEA
> By
> Louis Henry Sullivan

The nearest approach in America to this book of Professor Lethaby's is Architecture and democracy. Mr. Bragdon, besides being an architect, is an ornamentalist and a stage designer; he writes out of a deep conviction in a democracy which is still to come, and his hope is for an architecture which will

give it a suitable "shell." His collection of essays should be read in connection with The autobiography of an idea, by the late Louis Henry Sullivan. In this book, Mr. Sullivan set out to describe the process of an architect's education in America during the last half-century, and to show the encouragements and difficulties that attended an architect who sought to realize, in buildings, the spirit of American democracy. Mr. Sullivan himself was worsted in the struggle; ironically enough his own work is principally represented in small-town banks in the Middle West; but in his defeat he came to realize that architecture and civilization must develop hand in hand, and that if we want finer buildings, we must prepare the social soil for their growth. What chance is there of serving Democracy, if the architect must devote himself to opulent monuments, shrines, stock-exchanges, mansions, and tombs, whilst the mass of people work in industrial slums, and are housed by jerry-builders, who extract in profit "what the traffic will bear"?

These books will give the reader a sense of architecture as a living, contemporary thing—something that, at every turn, makes a profound and vital difference to him. Once this feeling has taken root, he will get much profit from consulting a standard

> A HISTORY OF
> ARCHITECTURE
> By Fiske Kimball
> and
> George Harold Edgell

This piece on architecture, written by Lewis Mumford, was reproduced as an exact facsimile in this Pentagram Paper.

No. 9: **Unilever House: Towards a New Ornament**

Back Story

A patron and friend to artists and craftspeople, partner Theo Crosby was instrumental in establishing London's Art & Architecture Group, which is dedicated to creating more humane and beautiful towns and cities. Restoring the interior of the Unilever House to its art deco splendor was just one of many important preservation commissions carried out by Crosby. Another noteworthy project was the reconstruction of Shakespeare's Globe Theatre, the original of which was built in 1599; Crosby devoted seventeen years to researching and authenticating every detail of the Globe for historical accuracy. He died in 1994, before the final phase was completed.

After completing the first phase of refurbishing the deco-inspired interior of London's landmark Unilever House in 1979, partner Theo Crosby paused to reflect on the scarcity of art and decoration in contemporary architecture and the remarkable difference they make when present.

Crosby took issue with critics who considered the Unilever House an "exemplar of everything the Modern Movement truly hated," and argued that current architecture "impoverished our complex urban inheritance. We have lost a natural poetry and feeling for place. . . . "

Crosby lamented that "building is now largely a process of assembly of finished components. Any intervention in the process causes delay and expense. Each component is progressively cheapened by being made in larger quantities and in blander forms, and variations are quietly dropped from production. Craftsmen become ever rarer and the assembly process becomes ever cruder."

Arguing that this did not have to be the case, Crosby provided close-up photographs of details in the Unilever House to show how contemporary craftspeople extrapolated elements found in the existing building to extend art deco themes in a fresh and convivial way.

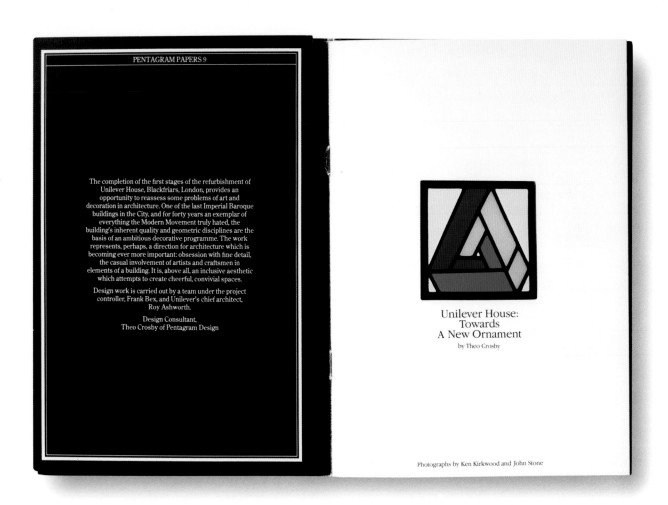

The completion of the first stages of the refurbishment of Unilever House, Blackfriars, London, provides an opportunity to reassess some problems of art and decoration in architecture. One of the last Imperial Baroque buildings in the City, and for forty years an exemplar of everything the Modern Movement truly hated, the building's inherent quality and geometric disciplines are the basis of an ambitious decorative programme. The work represents, perhaps, a direction for architecture which is becoming ever more important: obsession with fine detail, the casual involvement of artists and craftsmen in elements of a building. It is, above all, an inclusive aesthetic which attempts to create cheerful, convivial spaces.

Design work is carried out by a team under the project controller, Frank Bex, and Unilever's chief architect, Roy Ashworth.

Design Consultant,
Theo Crosby of Pentagram Design

Unilever House: Towards A New Ornament
by Theo Crosby

Photographs by Ken Kirkwood and John Stone

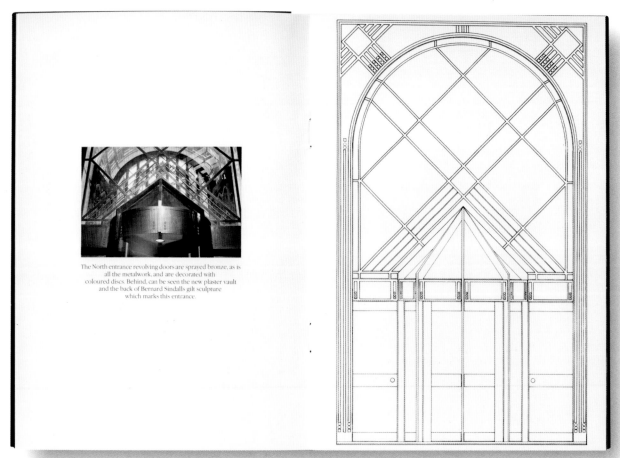

The North entrance revolving doors are sprayed bronze, as is all the metalwork, and are decorated with coloured discs. Behind, can be seen the new plaster vault and the back of Bernard Sindalls gilt sculpture which marks this entrance.

Saying that "to make a place for a craftsman is a blow for civilization . . . and runs counter to the process of current building," Theo Crosby made sure that sculptors and glass artists played an integral role in the refurbishment of the Unilever House.

Detail of the stair balustrade with enamelled vermilion discs connecting the cranked bronze verticals.

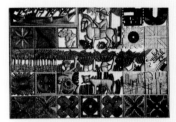

Chief Erhabor Emokpae of Benin carved the elaborate pieced timber relief which dominates the entrance hall. The gift of Unilever's subsidiary United Africa International, it represents Lord Leverhulme's African travels and enterprises.

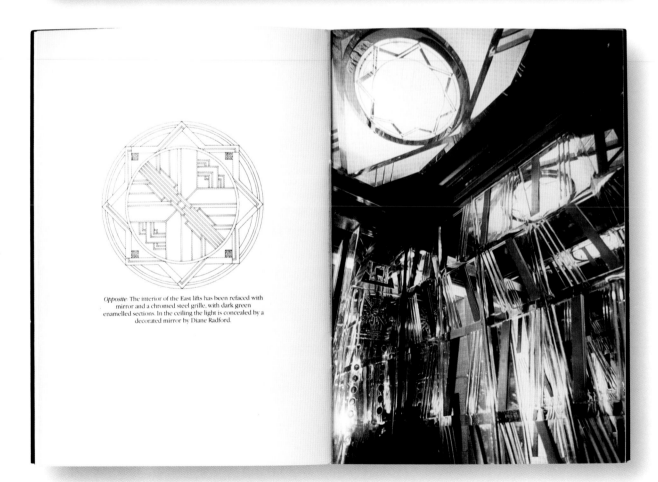

Opposite: The interior of the East lifts has been refaced with mirror and a chromed steel grille, with dark green enamelled sections. In the ceiling the light is concealed by a decorated mirror by Diane Radford.

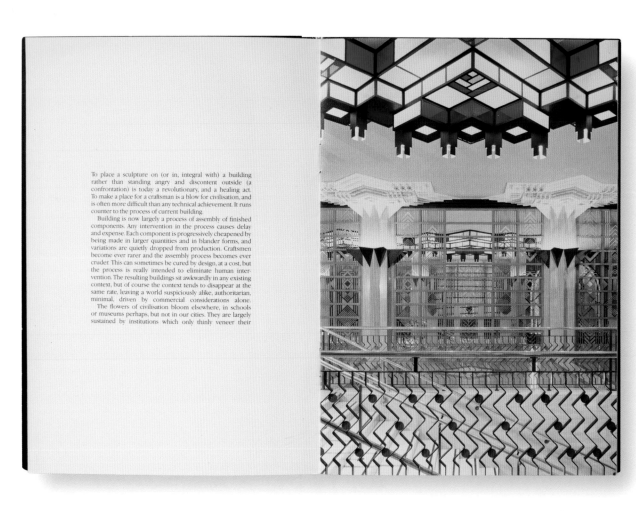

To place a sculpture on (or in, integral with) a building rather than standing angry and discontent outside (a confrontation) is today a revolutionary, and a healing act. To make a place for a craftsman is a blow for civilisation, and is often more difficult than any technical achievement. It runs counter to the process of current building.

Building is now largely a process of assembly of finished components. Any intervention in the process causes delay and expense. Each component is progressively cheapened by being made in larger quantities and in blander forms, and variations are quietly dropped from production. Craftsmen become ever rarer and the assembly process becomes ever cruder. This can sometimes be cured by design, at a cost, but the process is really intended to eliminate human intervention. The resulting buildings sit awkwardly in any existing context, but of course the context tends to disappear at the same rate, leaving a world suspiciously alike, authoritarian, minimal, driven by commercial considerations alone.

The flowers of civilisation bloom elsewhere, in schools or museums perhaps, but not in our cities. They are largely sustained by institutions which only thinly veneer their

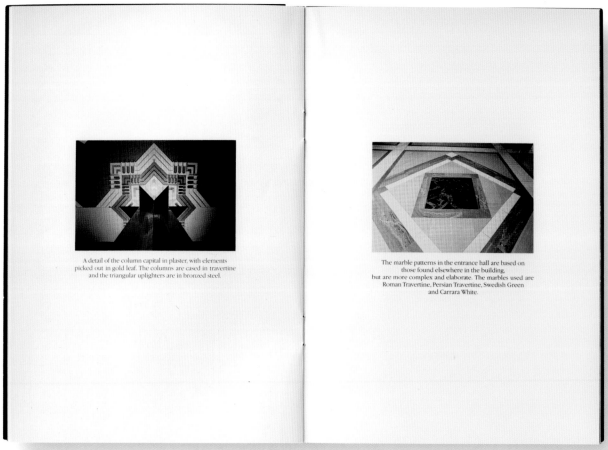

A detail of the column capital in plaster, with elements picked out in gold leaf. The columns are cased in travertine and the triangular uplighters are in bronzed steel.

The marble patterns in the entrance hall are based on those found elsewhere in the building, but are more complex and elaborate. The marbles used are Roman Travertine, Persian Travertine, Swedish Green and Carrara White.

For the Unilever House, contemporary craftspeople created original artwork rendered in stained glass, travertine marble, sprayed bronze, carved wood, and chromed steel.

A detail of Diane Radford's decorated mirror wall,
with oak framing. The decorative themes are an extrapolation
of elements found in the existing building.

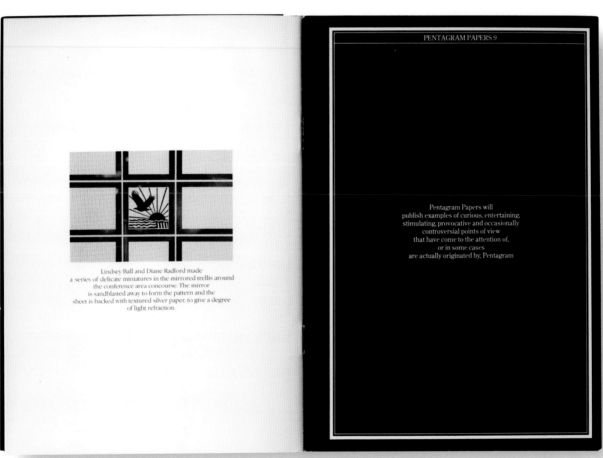

Lindsey Ball and Diane Radford made
a series of delicate miniatures in the mirrored trellis around
the conference area concourse. The mirror
is sandblasted away to form the pattern and the
sheet is backed with textured silver paper, to give a degree
of light refraction.

PENTAGRAM PAPERS 9

Pentagram Papers will
publish examples of curious, entertaining,
stimulating, provocative and occasionally
controversial points of view
that have come to the attention of,
or in some cases
are actually originated by, Pentagram

No. 12: **Olivier Mourgue's Little Theatre of Design**

In his workshop at his old stone farm-house near the sea on the north coast of Brittany, furniture and set designer Olivier Mourgue loves to spread his canvasses out on the floor and kneel down and paint on them. "Lightness—fragility, weightlessness—intrigues me," he says. "It appears to be related to intuition honed by experience. . . . A watercolor: paper, color, drops of water. I have been painting watercolors for years. I love the precision and the compelling need to coordinate body, breathing, concentration, and hand."

Mourgue populates his watercolor scenes with scattered objects—pebbles from the shore, driftwood, feathers, dried seaweed, children's drawings—and invents stories to bring life to his fanciful sets. Using small mirrors, he directs the last rays of sunset like spotlights to illuminate his "stage."

To share his creation with friends, Mourgue built a suitcase the size of a musical instrument case, which neatly holds all the sets and props and can travel easily by plane, taxi, or subway. Delighted audiences are enthralled by Mourgue's impromptu theater, which invites them into a world both playful and surreal.

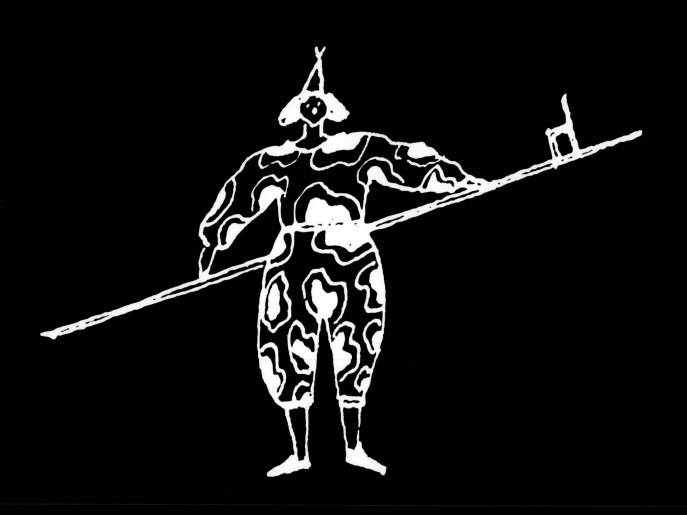

Kéralio, where we live, is an old stone farmhouse near the sea on the north coast of Brittany. It looks like a big boat set down in the middle of the fields. It is built of traditional Brittany materials, with a slate roof and walls of pink, grey-brown and black granite. Across the sky, often the greyish colour of oatmeal, sail white clouds. The sea is dark blue-grey; the islands off the coast are pink.

The vast workshop is black and white, timbered throughout with solid oak beams and posts. Two bow windows let in the daylight, and white cotton curtains stir in the sun. A tree from the garden has been sawn into planks, which are drying out. Animated canvasses, fringed with wool and decorated with tiny mirrors, are arranged with care across beams and rafters. My tools are lying in a neat row. The floor is on two levels. The lower level, in wood, gives on to the garden. There heavy tools, work benches and large paintings are stored. On the upper level, which has a wooden floor, I can spread out my canvasses as if I were a sailmaker and kneel down to draw and paint on them. Each area of the workshop has its own special purpose, for the changing light dictates what will be done and where. The children come here to work, and the cats snooze in the bow windows.

Lightness – fragility, weightlessness – intrigues me: it appears to be related to intuition honed by experience. It is fascinating to weigh the actual materials used in creative work. To paint a watercolour, for example, you need a sheet of paper, a few drops of water, paints of different colours and a brush. Their combined weight is perhaps only 13 grams yet the emotional force that they exert is incalculable. The same can be said of a 20-gram letter, feathers, kites . .

A watercolour: paper, colour, drops of water. I have been painting watercolours for years. I love the precision and the compelling need to co-ordinate body, breathing, concentration and hand. But watercolours

From a flat black suitcase, Olivier Mourgue pulls out everything he needs to construct his Little Theatre, including tiny front-row benches for his imaginary audience. Taking less than an hour to set up, the theater presents three silent and fanciful dramas.

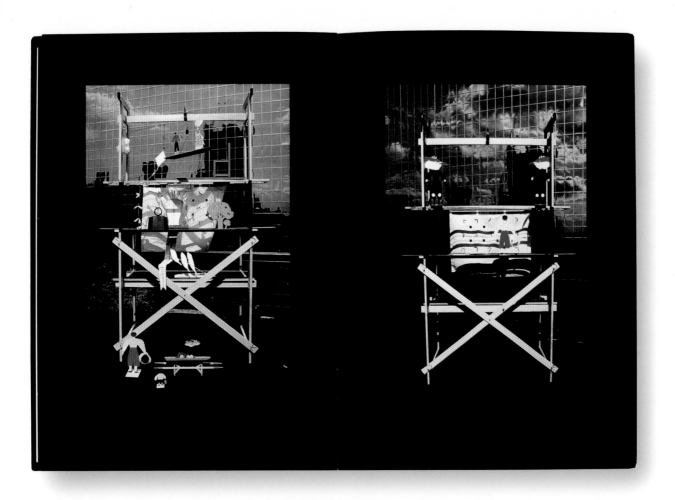

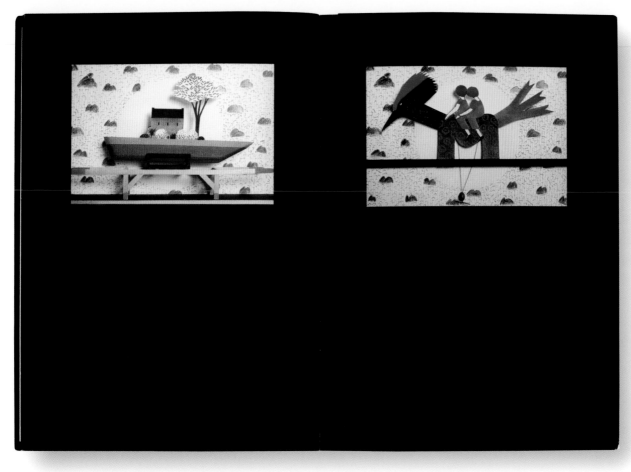

Olivier Mourgue's Little Theatre emerges as if from a dream. To tell his story, Mourgue creates props like watercolored paper actors, a boat with feathers for sails, pulleys to raise a kite, and a man sitting on a lounge chair in the water, reading a newspaper.

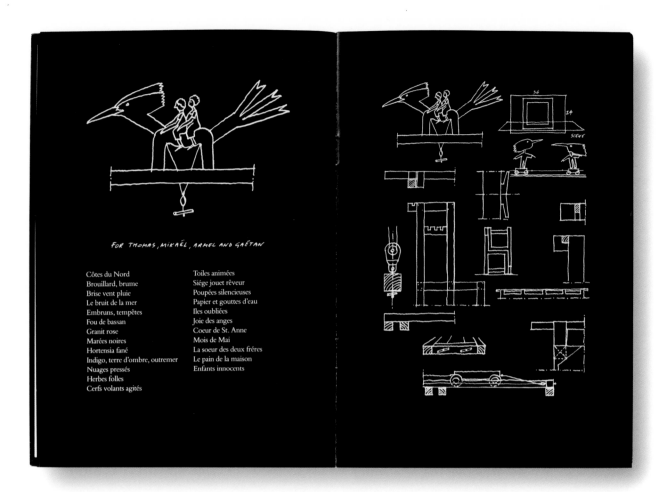

FOR THOMAS, MIKAËL, ARMEL AND GAÉTAN

Côtes du Nord
Brouillard, brume
Brise vent pluie
Le bruit de la mer
Embruns, tempêtes
Fou de bassan
Granit rose
Marées noires
Hortensia fané
Indigo, terre d'ombre, outremer
Nuages pressés
Herbes folles
Cerfs volants agités

Toiles animées
Siége jouet rêveur
Poupées silencieuses
Papier et gouttes d'eau
Iles oubliées
Joie des anges
Coeur de St. Anne
Mois de Mai
La soeur des deux frères
Le pain de la maison
Enfants innocents

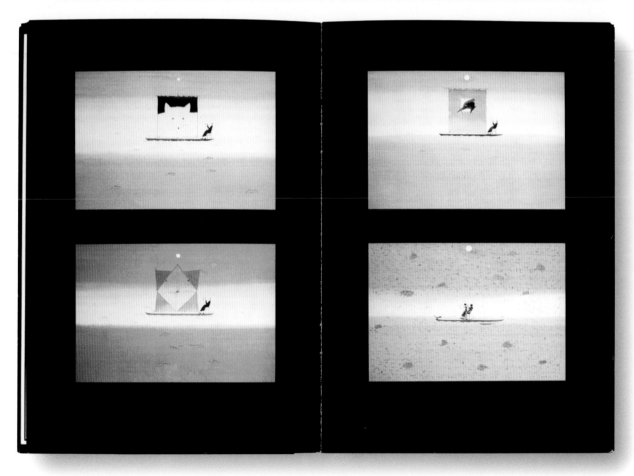

No. 26: **On Pride and Prejudice in the Arts**

Back Story

Sir Ernst Gombrich was eighty-three years old when he addressed a meeting of the Art & Architecture Group, which was founded on the initiative of partner Theo Crosby to promote collaboration between artists, craftspeople, and architects. One of Britain's most honored scholars, Gombrich was unparalleled in his knowledge and grasp of the history of the visual arts. The talk that he gave to the Art & Architecture gathering encapsulated many of the central arguments that he had posited during his distinguished career. Yet it was heard by only a select few. When a friend of Gombrich's family called Pentagram to suggest that the lecture merited broader exposure, partner John McConnell seized the opportunity to reprint it as a Pentagram Paper.

The most widely read art historian of the twentieth century, Sir Ernst Gombrich started his acclaimed book *The Story of Art* with the line, "There really is no such thing as art. There are only artists." His premise was that works of art, even those of Leonardo da Vinci, are created by craftsmen seeking solutions. For Gombrich, art was a skill or mastery that applied to science as much as painting.

In a 1992 address before London's Art & Architecture Group, which campaigns for enriching the built environment with art, Gombrich warned against indulging the vanities of artists and asked for renewed respect for the intrinsic humility and humanity of artisans. "The conviction has gained ground that anything an artist does is, *ipso facto*, art. I think it was Kurt Schwitters who said as much: 'I am an artist and when I spit it is art.'"

Gombrich rejected the artist's belief that "if he makes what are called 'concessions' to the taste of the client, he loses the respect of his fellow artists." He points out that the classic works of all time reveal the artisan's sensibility in innovating techniques, responding to the materials at hand, and considering the environment in which the creation would be viewed.

On Pride and Prejudice
in the Arts
SIR ERNST GOMBRICH, OM

I am an artist and when I spit it is art.

Now I can hardly imagine any one of you advocating that the next public building that goes up, should display near the entrance, a spittoon with Kurt Schwitters' spittle. Even less would I think that you would wish to be pilloried as philistines for not accepting this display as a gift from an enthusiastic sponsor. Naturally I have introduced this caricature to explain why I hope to bring the notions of pride and prejudice into this debate. If we desire a fruitful collaboration between the artist and the architect, we must first ask them both to swallow a bit of their pride and get rid of their ingrained prejudices, and that would be far from easy.

Personally, I came across this problem not exactly in the context that concerns you, but in the germane context of the well-being of the crafts today, when I was invited in 1991 to Faenza, that great centre of Renaissance pottery that gave its name to the term 'Fayence'. The occasion was an exhibition of contemporary pottery.[1] A number of well-known artists had been asked to collaborate with the local pottery workshops to produce new and contemporary designs as a development of these ancient traditions. I am not sure that the experiment was a total success, for though the dozen or more freelance artists who took part were obviously very willing to collaborate with these seasoned craftsmen, not all of them were able to adjust their inventions to the unfamiliar medium. What struck me in this laudable experiment was precisely how daring it looked, a full century after William Morris, even to suggest that an artist should forget his pride and accept a commission of this kind which normally he might have considered to be below his

dignity. It was then that I began to realise that we were confronted with what I should call a moral problem, a question of ethics and I said so in a little speech for that occasion. Even in such a renowned centre of excellence as Faenza, the crafts always had to respond to the laws of demand and supply. Indeed, it was these laws that drove their workshops to emulate the choicest products of tableware and to surpass them in refinement and durability. The craftsman, the artisan, thus existed and only could exist in the social nexus of give-and-take and whatever his personal attitude, he had to practise the virtue of humility in his response to the market on which his livelihood depended, a humility to learn from others and to accept the demands of the client without demur.

It is here that I see the fateful gulf between the artisan and the artist. For the code of ethics adopted by artists rejects the virtue of humility as if it were the worst of all vices. The artist has to be a law unto himself. He has to cultivate his own personality and, if he makes what are called 'concessions' to the taste of the client, he loses the respect of his fellow artists. Thus the gulf that began to open in certain periods of history between the artisan and the artist seems to me of a moral nature. Insisting to be the favourite of the Muse, if not the mouthpiece of divine powers, the creative artist will have no truck with the common crowd. Remember the opening of the fourth ode by Horace:

Odi profanum vulgus et arceo. – I hate the profane crowd and I keep it at bay.[2]

'Profanum vulgus' are the uninitiated outside the precincts of the sanctuary whom the poet wants to keep at bay. Fair

[2]   [3]

While Sir Ernst Gombrich's books have been read by people around the world, his talk to the London Art & Architecture Group was heard by a few dozen people. Reprinting his presentation allowed his words to reach a broader audience.

114 Personal Passions

enough, but must he also hate them? What harm have they done him? Is any human being entitled to feel so superior over the majority of his fellow creatures? I suppose I should warn you that this is only the first of a good many texts I propose to refer to. Texts are the testimonies on which the historians have to rely, unless they prefer to deconstruct them, which I don't.

I want to remind you of a text that suggests that even during the Middle Ages, which our romantics so like to idealise, pride and arrogance was said to be the besetting sin of artists. I am referring to the episode in Dante's *Divine Comedy* where the poet is taken through purgatory to witness the penance of those who still have the hope of salvation.[3] The souls of those who were guilty of the sin of pride are here seen carrying heavy loads on their backs which bend their proud necks. One of them is recognised by Dante, who addresses him:

Are you not Oderisi di Gubbio who was the honour of the art which in Paris they call illumination?

But the penitent now knows better than to accept this compliment.

The honour is due to another painter. To Franco Bolognese who deserved it more, for the pages he painted looked more cheerful, they smiled more. True, when I was alive I would never have admitted so much, so great was the desire to excel that filled my heart; it is for this ambition that now one has to pay the price.

After which the miniature painter launches on to a little

sermon about the futility of ambition and the vanity of human glory. The passage has remained famous because it states as his example, none other than his contemporary – Giotto.

Cimabue thought he was the best painter, but who remembers him now? Everybody talks of Giotto. What matter? Human glory is no better than a puff of wind that blows from one side and then from another and changes names as it changes direction.

It is a strange irony of fate that this sermon against the vanity of earthly fame became the source and origin of Giotto's fame, who is still not forgotten, however often the wind changes direction. A generation after Dante, Giovanni Boccaccio[4] also gave reasons for Giotto's enduring fame by linking him with what we now call 'The Renaissance', the rebirth of the arts. It was Giotto, he claimed, 'who brought back to life the art of painting that had been lost, lost because of the error of those who preferred to feast the eye of the ignorant rather than to do justice to reason.' So if Dante introduces us to the sin of pride among artists, Boccaccio helps me to focus on the prejudice with which Western civilization has had to contend ever since: Pleasure, which means of course sensual pleasure, is corrupting. For an artist to try to please the ignorant is the road to perdition. Soon afterwards a Florentine chronicler[5] assures us that Giotto never descended so low. He always preferred fame to gain.

Mark what this formula implies that has remained a cliché in our tradition: to strive for gain, for 'filthy lucre' as we say, is unworthy of the artist, for he can only make money if he

pleases the ignorant multitude. In trying to do so, he will lose the right to be remembered by posterity, his claim to fame. This conviction may be called the foundation stone of Western artistic ethics. It was probably the first thing a young apprentice artist learnt on entering an academy and it may still be haunting our art schools today. I need hardly remind you of the presence of this tradition in the Discourses of Sir Joshua Reynolds to which I also had to refer when giving the Reynolds lecture at the Royal Academy in 1990. I like to read these Discourses because of the good sense they contain, but also for the constant reminder of how things have changed. They have changed because Reynolds is never plagued by doubts. He is convinced of the hierarchy of values he inherited, the very hierarchy for which the pleasure which art can give, stands lowest on the scales. It stands low because it appeals to the groundlings, to the vulgar, who have no better criterion than pleasure. But let me quote a passage that illustrates both the prejudice and the pride.

It is certain that the lowest style will be the most popular as it falls within the compass of ignorance itself and the vulgar will always be pleased with what is natural in the confused and misunderstood sense of the word.

He is referring to Dutch seventeenth-century painting.

One would wish that such depravation of taste should be counteracted with that manly pride which actuated Euripides when he said to the Athenians who criticised his works. 'I do not compose my works in order to be

corrected by you, but to instruct you.' It is true, to have a right to speak thus a man must be a Euripides. However, this much may be allowed, that when an artist is sure that he is upon firm ground, supported by the authority and practice of his predecessors he may then assume the boldness of the greatest reputation and intrepidity of genius. At any rate he must not be tempted out of the right path by the allurement of popularity which always accompanies the lower styles of painting.[6]

But the first President of the Academy was too worldly-wise not to see the dangers of the doctrine he preached. It is all right, he knew, to refrain from flattering the senses, but the artist must not be tempted by pride to go to the other extreme. I quote:

When simplicity, instead of being a corrector seems to be set up for herself, that is when an artist seems to value himself solely upon this quality, such an ostentatious display of simplicity becomes then as disagreeable and nauseous as any other kind of affectation. He is however, in this case likely enough, to sit down contented with his own work for though he finds the world looks at it with indifference or dislike, as being destitute of every quality that can recreate or give pleasure to the mind, yet he consoles himself that it has simplicity, a beauty of too pure and too chaste a nature to be relished by vulgar minds.[7]

Now I am sure that the academic doctrine of the true road to fame would not have had such an appeal if it had been

No. 16: **Kingswalden Notes**

Back Story

While working on a project with a London property developer, partner John McConnell was introduced to the classical architect Quinlan Terry, who showed him a journal he kept while working on Kings Walden Bury. Terry's drawings and handwritten notes provided a rare glimpse of a young man arriving at insights that would become the driving force of his career. This was the period of change when Terry's philosophy took root. McConnell got permission to reproduce *Kingswalden Notes* in full because he felt it revealed the thinking of one of the twentieth century's most ardent champions of classical architecture.

A leading figure in the revival of classical architecture, English architect Quinlan Terry has emphasized the use of traditional materials, construction methods, and symbolic ornaments. His dedication to remaining true to the lineage of classical design began early in his career while he was under the tutelage of his renowned mentor and partner, Raymond Erith. He went on to design staterooms in 10 Downing Street, and Merchant Square at Colonial Williamsburg in Virginia, among other commissions.

As a young man in his early thirties, Terry received his first major commission: to design and build Kings Walden Bury, a new country house in Hertfordshire, England. During its construction between 1969 and 1971, he meticulously recorded his research, drawings, and observations in a journal, *Kingswalden Notes*, and expressed his passionate feelings on classicism and its worldly context—social, moral, and theological. Terry remained steadfast in this commitment, even knowing he was swimming against the tides. As he closed out his journal, he wrote: ". . . we can see very quickly why the Moderns prefer to keep away from an art which has to be a labour of love. But like everything we love, we love it for a good reason. It may become a consuming passion but it never loses its interest and as we grow older, our capacity to enjoy it becomes greater."

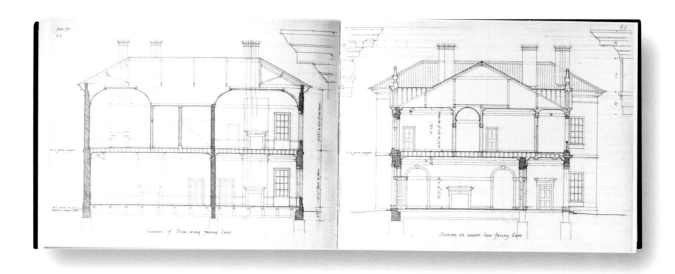

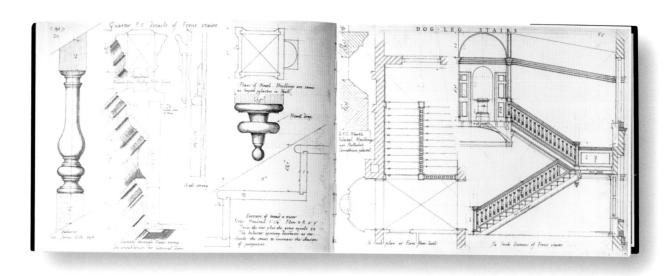

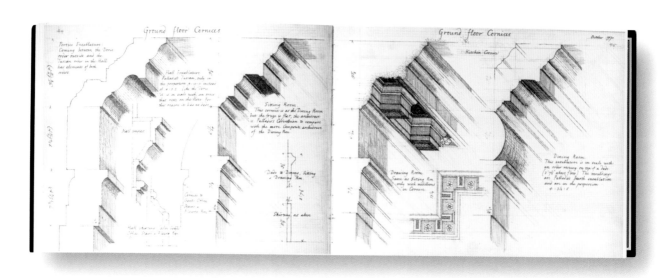

In keeping with the horizontal format of Quinlan Terry's original journal, this Pentagram Paper is printed landscape style. Terry's beautifully rendered drawings give exact measurements for every detail.

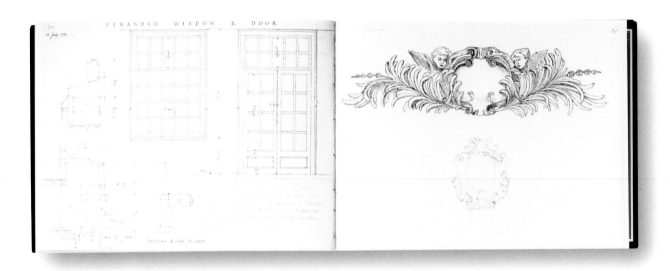

The photograph of the finished Kings Walden Bury house, shown on page 117, reveals just how closely Terry adhered to his original vision, as seen in the drawing at the top of this page.

No. 2: **The Pessimist Utopia**

Back Story

Born in South Africa in 1925, partner Theo Crosby moved to London in 1947, setting up a private practice while also serving as technical editor of *Architectural Design* magazine. Early on, he became known for award-winning exhibitions, including the British section of the Milan Triennale of 1964, for which he won a Gran Premio, *L'Idée et la Forme*, and an exhibition of British design at the Louvre in 1971. In the latter half of his career, Crosby became an active preservationist, vociferously arguing that modern trends were creating a sterile, faceless city and speaking out on behalf of reintegrating ornamental art and handicraft into architecture.

In an address to the Royal College of Art in London in 1975, Theo Crosby, architect and Pentagram partner, argued for the need to reintegrate the contributions of artists and craftsmen into architecture. Crosby contended that many of today's commercial buildings left the public cold.

It is not the use of new materials or the current visual language that the public spurned, but the intellectual attitude, Crosby said. "[Crude and ugly structures] intrude clumsily into every town and landscape. But, above all, they are given; handed down to us by a conspiracy of committees, experts, architects, and developers, and we have no say in their form or content. The new buildings represent a world of faceless authority, which cannot be influenced or exchanged, and to whom responsibility cannot be pinned. We do not identify ourselves or our lives with these buildings, because they belong to nobody, they are designed and built by nobody."

In arguing the case for personalizing commercial buildings through art, Crosby explained that "great art is welcome" because "the artist's role is to assert the tangible, the tactile, the human scale, to provide complexity in detail; to give some life, humor, and amusement to our pompous buildings."

It is precisely this domination, this kind of insidious diffusion into our mental structures, that Pugin and Ruskin so feared and against which they wrote and argued. But already in the work of Morris, and later with Ashbee and Lethaby the process of accommodation to the industrial process becomes more and more apparent.

Industry is concerned with logic and order, and with organisation. The organisation that was available to be adapted, that was capable of dealing with large quantities, was the military structure. One might say that the battle for industrial supremacy was won on the field of Waterloo.

The modern movement was the result, not so much of an accommodation with industrial thinking, which Lethaby had promoted, but an open acceptance of industrial values. The hope and intention was to drag a new kind of poetry from this system, to conquer the machine through design.

Designers therefore forswore the roughness (the very carefully cultivated roughness) of the hand worked surfaces which had been the hallmark of the avant garde; and accepted the perfection of the machine finish. Thus within a few years after the turn of the century the position of the design avant garde was reversed, and the basic, anti-industrial theories of the 19th century rejected.

We might try to make a list of the imperatives underlying the modern movement, and consider whether they are still relevant.

We live in a mass society
Economy of scale
Bigger is better
Man at the centre
Form follows function
History is bunk
Art is not decoration; and decoration is not art
The city is evil
Universal mobility
Sincerity is more important than mere beauty
The expert knows best

There are many, many more of these phrases and they form a kind of collective unconscious which predicates certain actions, and guarantees their automatic acceptance. Thus in the name of universal mobility we accept (with a little regret) the destruction of our cities by new roads. We accept vast new developments because bigger is better, and anyway cheaper, and that must be morally right. That this (actually very dubious)

4

Is bigger always, or even occasionally, better?
St Pancras Station.

Should form always follow function?
Daily Telegraph Building, Fleet Street.

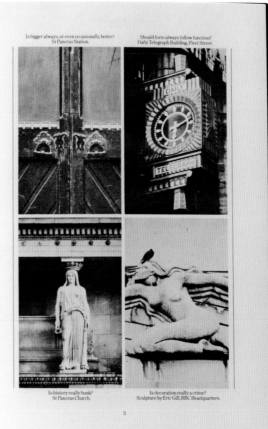

Is history really bunk?
St Pancras Church.

Is decoration really a crime?
Sculpture by Eric Gill, BBC Headquarters.

5

and the dwellings would be maintained partly by the market pressure, and perhaps partly by a building lease system which gives some elementary landlord controls to local authorities.

There is no necessity for our vast housing departments which cannot by their inner natures, and will not, from their expert convictions, work simply and directly in relation to the people who occupy their buildings. In the end the only possible, satisfactory relationship is that between a willing, careful buyer, and a willing seller, or provider of services. The pessimist will always beware of anyone bearing gifts. He will therefore encourage, ensure, the independence of the consumer, and aim to establish an equal relationship between the architect and his patron. We have spent many years taxing away income differentials, and are now all paid much more evenly paid than, for example, Communist China. It is time to draw a social conclusion. We are equal, more or less. Why should we not equally command our individual houses to suit our needs? Why not employ architects to make our individual houses, rather than pack them like battery hens into plan factories. In the end the processes of industrialisation rule in all large organisations; in housing they create hierarchies, bureaucracy, and overheads.

The identity of the individual
is sustained by unique architecture.
It's available at every scale.

14

They are also extremely expensive, make large expensive mistakes, and can seldom be reached by either logic or emotion.

Now, of course I don't expect the GLC housing department to commit suicide tomorrow, though I hear they are getting a little worried about their product. But they could try a game, a strategy from the pessimist utopia. For the next batch of 200 houses, to which they would provide a team of say 20 architects, they could select 200 families from the housing list. Each architect would be allocated 10 families and would be expected to produce what they required. Each family would be offered a mortgage, and a building lease and a site. Within that budget they should be able to choose their own spaces, standards of finish, everything — just as if they were real human beings. If they wanted more space, and were prepared to do their own decorating, or even their own buildings, that would be their decision.

In this way the consumer would be strengthened, would accept and enjoy the responsibility and share the pleasures of the housing process.

The administrative device required for this strategy is simply the separation of the design responsibility from the financial provision. It is because these two strands have become so interwoven, a relic of the

15

For Theo Crosby, preserving the humanity of an urban environment through the thoughtful merging of architecture, design, and art was an ardent crusade. He manifested this belief in his architectural commissions.

engineer's idea of amenity, crazy paving and badly designed flower pots.

Here at least is a setting for civic art, touched by, and immediately accessible to the public. We should organise a nationwide competition to provide in each town sculptures, fountains or murals to fill, to ornament these newly discovered, impatiently waiting spaces.

Nevertheless the essential is the personal relation between a producer and a consumer who wants the product. As Bemelmans said the only thing more pleasurable than painting a picture is selling it.

For the arts to survive requires changes in attitudes and above all in public policies. Artists have tried to maintain avant garde attitudes in the face of an ever increasing demand for, and knowledge of art, in order to maintain the fiction which sees the artist always as a special kind of person. As public knowledge of art has grown we have tried to maintain an intellectual superiority over ever decreasing territories. There is now hardly any territory left; art has ceased to be physical, because the physical can be explained, and compared, and criticised, and become conceptual.

The time has come, therefore, to move in another direction, perhaps in the direction to which architecture and planning are now moving. Towards a more realist, user oriented role, where the professional sees himself more a servant and interpreter than an organiser or disposer of people's lives. Most architects now regret their years of concern with purely formal problems, their acceptance of an easy, shallow system without much thought for the social consequences.

In the same way the promoters and organisers of art in the past twenty years have seen exhibitions as a creative opportunity, with the artists work as the raw material to be shaped into a movement, or juxtaposed to prove a point. Rather than exhibitions geared to the needs of the organisers' creativity, or to bait the critics, or to our inherent literary bias, we need a more intelligent way of bringing artists before the public; and one that will outflank the commercial galleries that control the business.

If we are to have a more equal society through the blessings of taxation, then the state must accept a responsibility for the support of the arts, and artists. It must set up and staff an alternative gallery system, where work can be shown without much anxiety or stress, and on a scale that matches the numbers of artists now working in this country. The Serpentine Gallery is an excellent precedent. A more important ploy would be to partially and secretly subsidise apparently com-

20

Art acts as a mediator between architect and consumer.

21

An incidental benefit of a more labour intensive economy.

6

economy is some sharp individual's private gain is somehow seen as not so much a social loss (which it is) but more a demonstration of the benefits of a free society.

We can see, now, that many of these basic assumptions have turned out to be counter-productive. They were based on a series of intellectual propositions and economic conditions which no longer seem to apply with such force. For example, the desacralisation of the world, which is implied by the phrase 'man at the centre' might have been a good idea in a world engaged in religious wars. Today the resultant boredom with anything intangible or spiritual is entirely negative. We have been robbed of a dimension.

At another level, a hundred years of cheap fuel has produced a set of assumptions about building which must now be radically revised; and which, incidentally, now present a formidable intellectual and technological challenge.

At present our heating, lighting, transport, industry and agriculture, our whole complicated civilisation, depends on cheap oil. We have structured our affluent lives on a resource which no one expects will last more than twenty years at the current rate of extraction. Most of the oil is consumed in Europe and North America. The problem of adaptation to other technologies is going, therefore, to be most urgent and traumatic in the west.

For the architect the new fuel equation prefigures a kind of building very different from present practice. Much of our technology will be simply abandoned – tall buildings, for example, use disproportionately more energy in construction and servicing. Buildings will become heavier, and will be expected to last a good deal longer. In effect we would tend to revert to earlier systems, more labour intensive, but less wasteful of fuel and material.

The idea of a more labour intensive building process opens at once certain possibilities that were renounced by the theorists fifty years ago.

We can now see that the vocabulary of the modern movement was the result of a number of social, technical and economic factors which coincided at a moment in time, about 1925. History was rewritten to prove the inevitability of the mainstream modern movement, and its postwar success is a tribute to a very successful process of education.

Since 1940 every art and architecture student has been trained within this new orthodoxy, and everything built or thought since that time carries the stamp of the modern movement. Though much has been

7

Collections

Collectors can be divided into two categories: Those who seek out beautiful objects like Monet paintings and Ming vases that are precious, rare, and monetarily valuable, and those who are drawn to collecting everyday things that individually may be worth little but are fascinating for their diversity within a given category. A single broom is merely a commonplace tool, but five hundred different brooms allow intriguing comparisons of materials, size, shape, purpose, cultural habits, historical changes, and the like. This latter kind of collecting is a study in form and function, graphic solutions, and cultural expression that many designers find compelling because it hones their ability to note the variations and distinctiveness of like objects.

No. 4: **Face to Face**

Imagination is an exercise in seeing what others often fail to see. That was the case with Swiss designer Jean Edouard Robert and his brother, photographer François, who saw accidental faces in objects of all kind. Faces were staring back at them from everywhere—light switches, envelopes, belt buckles, cardboard boxes, shoes, and purses. The "expressions" ranged from surprise and jubilation to sadness and sheepishness. Since the 1970s, the Robert brothers—first Jean and later François—have photographed more than one thousand of these hidden faces and have published five books on the subject. The photographs, along with the actual objects, have also been exhibited in shows in Europe. Interestingly, the Robert brothers have observed that when people are shown the photographs collectively, they have little trouble spotting the faces; but, conversely, they become so fixated on the face that they have trouble identifying what the actual object is.

While working at Pentagram in London, Jean Edouard Robert started photographing accidental faces to amuse himself and friends, but the exercise soon drew public demand to see more.

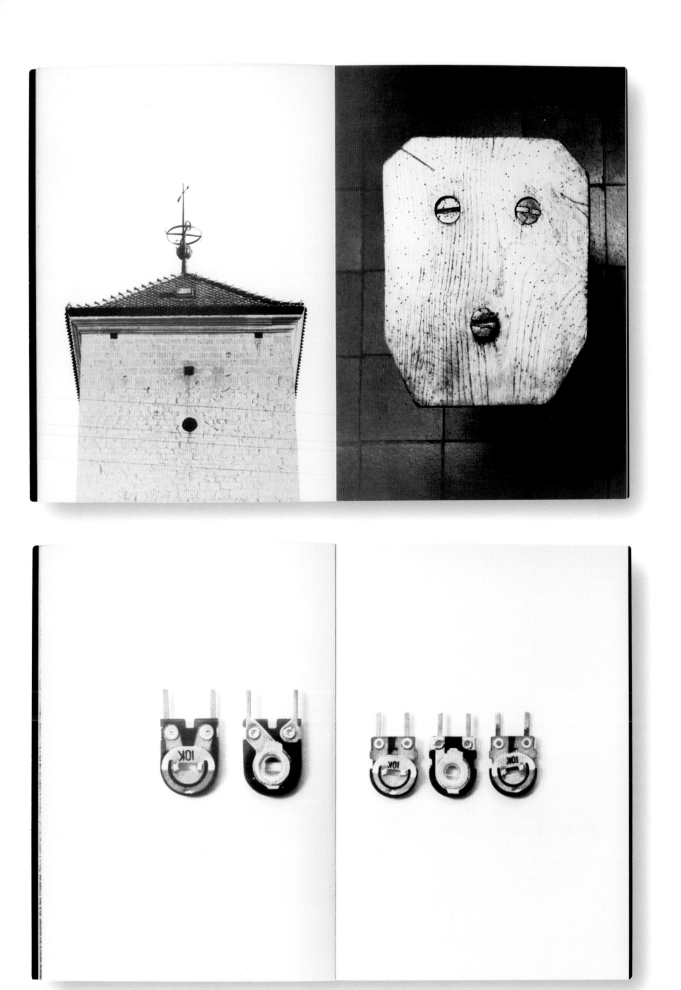

Enlisted to help his brother, François recalls, "When I visited Jean, he'd send me home to Chicago with a suitcase full of face objects to photograph. I'd have to schlep them across the ocean to my studio."

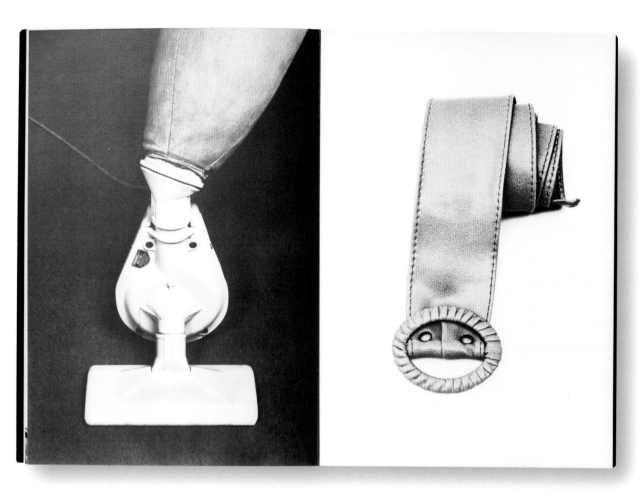

Photographer François Robert says he now finds that faces stare back at him from all kinds of places. He says jokingly, "Faces look at me and say, 'Please take my picture. Immortalize me, François.'"

No. 14: **Stars & Stripes**

The most recognizable national symbol in the world today, the American flag embodies the ethos of the nation. People have loved it, hated it, sworn allegiance to it, fought for it, and died for it. It has been hoisted on the moon and on battlefields, saluted in respect, and burned in protest. The evocative power of the flag makes it far more than a mere pattern of stars and stripes rendered in red, white, and blue. Rich in patriotic meaning, the national banner has appeared on everything from soup cans, decorative pillows, belt buckles, and weather vanes to folding fans, campaign buttons, and homemade quilts. The many interpretations of the Stars and Stripes are partly due to the fact that no official design guidelines existed for the flag until after 1912—when the last star of the forty-eight continental United States was added. That left professional flag makers and average citizens free to impose their personal taste on the size, shape, and placement of stars and the width of the stripes. The wide range of interpretations provides a unique and fascinating perspective on American culture and the times.

The American flags shown here are a small portion of the more than 400 flag artifacts collected over the past 20 years by Kit Hinrichs, a Pentagram partner in the San Francisco office. Kit's interest in the Stars and Stripes was whetted by an heirloom hand-sewn woolen flag made by his great-great-great aunt in Ohio in 1865. This 36-star banner, grown fragile over the generations, was unfurled every Independence Day for more than a century, and forms the cornerstone of the collection. What's evident in this assembly of flag ephemera and folk art is that Americans have treated their national emblem with an affectionate familiarity. Like the feisty, white-bearded Uncle Sam, Old Glory has been more than a symbol, it's a personification of the American spirit.

Photography by Barry Robinson. Written by Delphine Hirasuna. Typography by Reardon & Krebs.

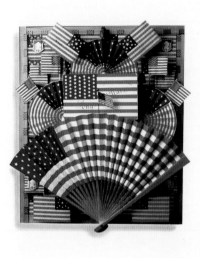

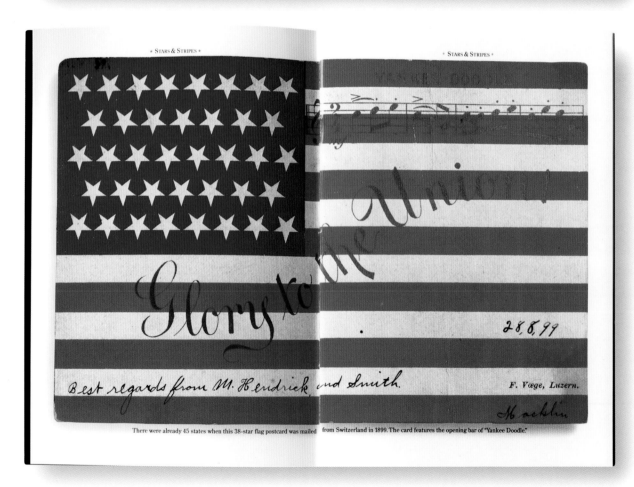

There were already 45 states when this 38-star flag postcard was mailed from Switzerland in 1899. The card features the opening bar of "Yankee Doodle."

The Stars and Stripes is the only national flag that has change built into it, through the addition of a star each time a state is inducted into the Union. There have been twenty-seven official flags since the nation's inception.

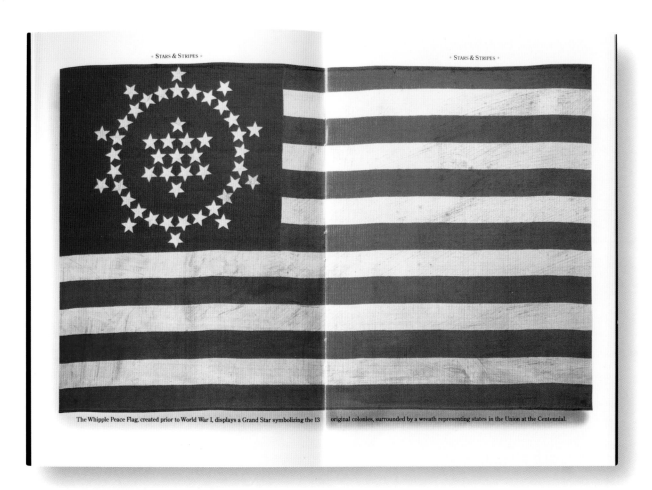

The Whipple Peace Flag, created prior to World War I, displays a Grand Star symbolizing the 13 original colonies, surrounded by a wreath representing states in the Union at the Centennial.

The Stars and Stripes have appeared in every art medium, including decaled on glass against a background of inlaid butterfly wings. Americans used the flag so loosely in commercial advertising that in 1942

Congress passed restrictive flag codes. The Old Glory brand symbol is just one of many uses that became outlawed. The codes forbade displaying the flag for advertising purposes, on cushions and handkerchiefs, or with any writing or design upon it.

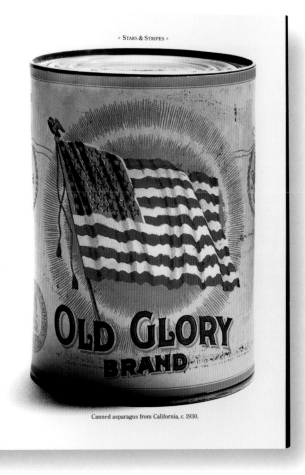

Canned asparagus from California, c. 1930.

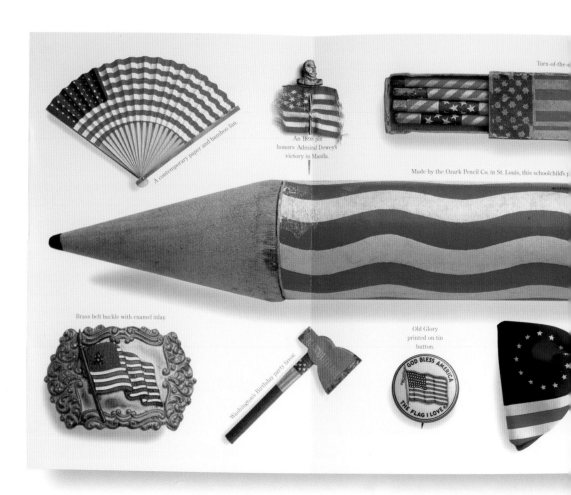

A contemporary paper and bamboo fan.

An 1898 pin honors Admiral Dewey's victory in Manila.

Turn-of-the-

Made by the Ozark Pencil Co. in St. Louis, this schoolchild's p

Brass belt buckle with enamel inlay.

Washington's Birthday party favor.

Old Glory printed on tin button.

GOD BLESS AMERICA
THE FLAG I LOVE

Over the last two hundred years, Americans have fondly displayed the colors of Old Glory on all kinds of novelty items. Respect for the flag hasn't precluded treating the national emblem with a bit of whimsy.

Made in post-war Japan, cigar band flags ingeniously collapsed inward into their hollow cores. When folded, they looked just like regular cigars.

Enterprising merchants have found all kinds of ways to wrap their product around the American flag, including on paper cigar fans, belt buckles, cigarette felts, spoons, and pencil boxes, to name a few things.

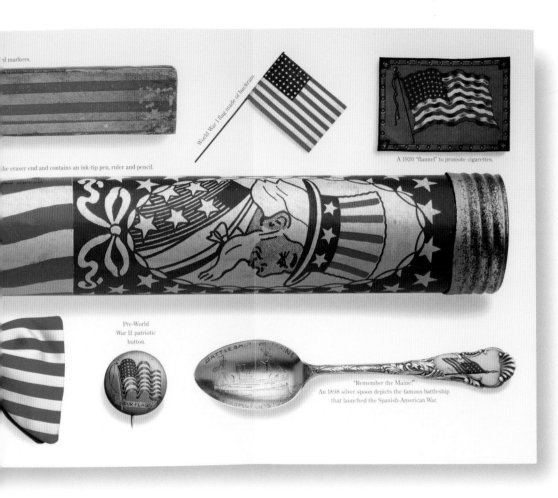

...d markers.

...he eraser end and contains an ink-tip pen, ruler and pencil.

World War I flag made of buckram.

A 1920 "flannel" to promote cigarettes.

Pre-World War II patriotic button.

OUR FLAG

"Remember the Maine!"
An 1898 silver spoon depicts the famous battleship
that launched the Spanish-American War.

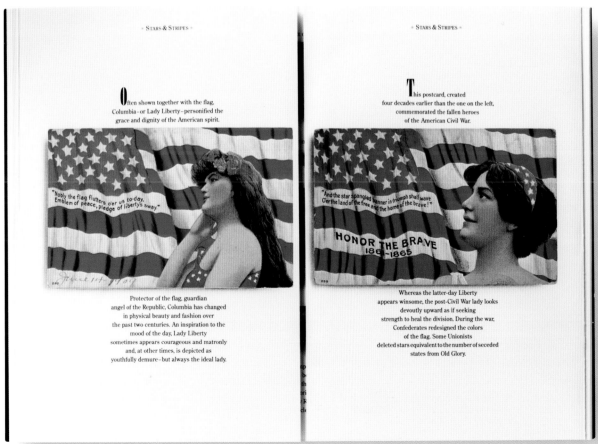

Often shown together with the flag,
Columbia–or Lady Liberty–personified the
grace and dignity of the American spirit.

"Nobly the flag flutters o'er us to-day,
Emblem of peace, pledge of liberty's sway."

Protector of the flag, guardian
angel of the Republic, Columbia has changed
in physical beauty and fashion over
the past two centuries. An inspiration to the
mood of the day, Lady Liberty
sometimes appears courageous and matronly
and, at other times, is depicted as
youthfully demure–but always the ideal lady.

This postcard, created
four decades earlier than the one on the left,
commemorated the fallen heroes
of the American Civil War.

"And the star spangled banner in triumph shall wave
O'er the land of the free and the home of the brave!"

HONOR THE BRAVE
186 -1865

Whereas the latter-day Liberty
appears winsome, the post-Civil War lady looks
devoutly upward as if seeking
strength to heal the division. During the war,
Confederates redesigned the colors
of the flag. Some Unionists
deleted stars equivalent to the number of seceded
states from Old Glory.

Even after thirty-five years of collecting, Hinrichs says he keeps finding Stars and Stripes objects that he hasn't seen before.

No. 18: **Skeleton Closet**

For centuries, Western cultures have believed that the eternal, formless soul is the most significant element of human life, but as far back as 5000 B.C., man has left indications of his enduring fascination with the final, physical evidence of life—the skeleton. In ritual and decorative arts, the skeleton has been depicted at various times as morbid or merry, awful and awesome. The skull and crossbones became the emblem of pirates and villains who wished to strike terror in their enemies, and the warning symbol of dangers such as poison and peril. For Shakespeare, the skull was a reminder of the transitory qualities of earthly pleasure. For modern bikers and low-riders, it has come to represent reckless machismo. But nowhere in the world has the human skeleton been more celebrated than Latin America, where it serves as a joyous remembrance of departed ancestors in annual Day of the Dead (*El Día de los Muertos*) festivities held on November 2. An entire genre of folk art has emerged around *El Día de los Muertos*, including festive decorations, masks, pins, pottery, candy, toys, and figurines.

Skeleton Closet

People in western cultures have believed for centuries that the eternal, formless soul is the most significant element of human life. But as far back as 5000 B.C., man has left indications of his enduring fascination with the final, physical evidence of life – the skeleton.

Anatomically, the skeleton is a spectacular piece of architecture; it is made up of 206 named bones, each one specialized in shape, function and composition.

In the ritual and decorative art of the world, the skeleton appears both morbid and merry, awful and awesome.

A long-standing emblem for criminals and pirates, the skull and cross-bones also represent many black and frightening concepts in our society: poison, danger, death and decay. The skeleton haunts our Halloweens and stars in our splatter films.

In stark contrast, The Day of the Dead in Mexico is a joyous remembrance of departed ancestors. *El Dia de los Muertos* has resulted in an entire genre of folk art comprised of decorations, masks, pins, pottery, candy, toys, and figurines in which the skeleton is represented not menacingly, but amusingly.

An accomplished illustrator and long-time friend of Pentagram, Steven Guarnaccia recently gave an informal talk in our New York office about his unusual collections of toys and books. One of the most interesting sub-collections centers on the skeleton theme. In the following pages, we are pleased to share with you a sampling of his remarkable and diverse collection.

Woody Pirtle

Steven Guarnaccia's collection of the skeletal form includes toys, functional objects, and art prints from all over the world.

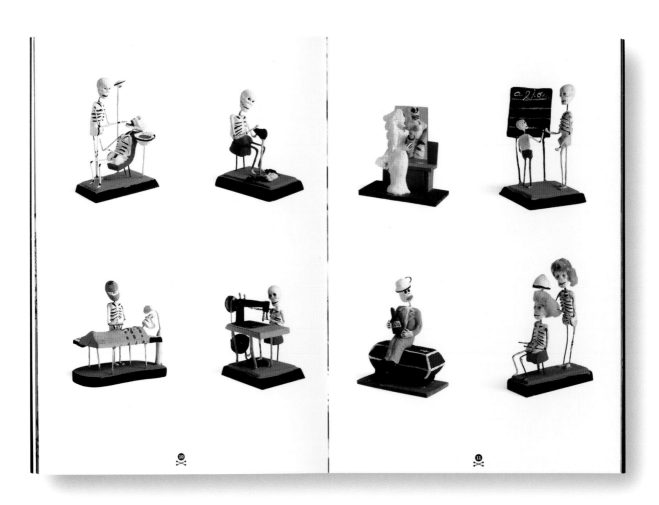

Like the folk art produced for Day of the Dead celebrations in Mexico, many of the skeleton objects created by contemporary artists are given animate personalities and are even shown in everyday life settings.

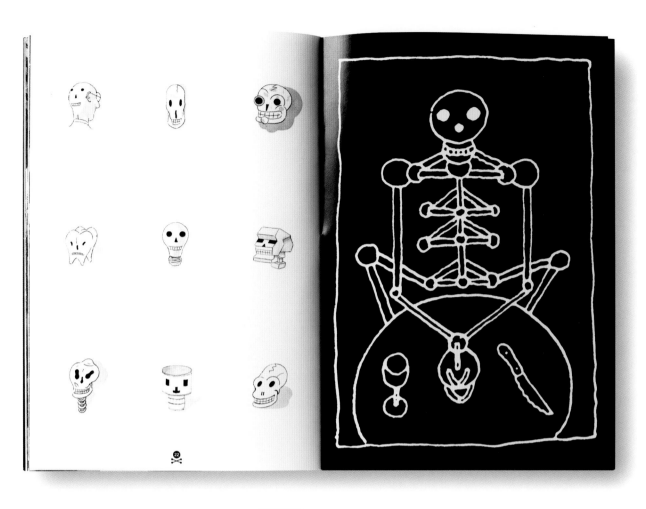

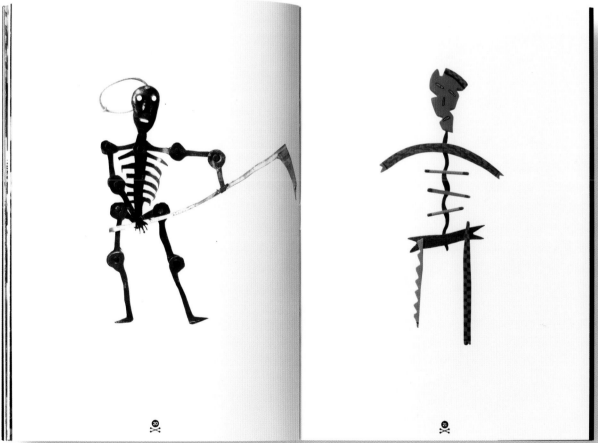

Guarnaccia not only collects skeleton objects, he draws them, as seen in the playful illustrations at the top of this page.

No. 25: **Souvenir Albums**

The introduction of affordable little souvenir albums in the late nineteenth century exposed everyday people to the world beyond their neighborhood. In the United States, the appearance of such albums coincided with the completion of the transcontinental railroad in 1869 and the Centennial celebration in 1876. Americans clamored for pictures of places they had visited and sought images of historic national achievements to display in their parlors. With halftone printing and hand-held cameras yet to be invented, publishers in the United States collaborated with printers in Germany to transform photographs into stone lithographic reproductions. Between 1870 and 1900, this roundabout method resulted in thousands of souvenir albums featuring landmarks, scenic views, and historic events. These miniature booklets, sold in railroad depots, luggage shops, and stationery stores, made it possible for people who may not have ventured more than fifty miles from home to view the wonders of the world. They also gave land developers a way to sell the attractions of remote places. New printing technology and the introduction of the Kodak Brownie box camera in 1900, which allowed people to take their own snapshots, led to the quick demise of monotinted souvenir albums.

[EXOTIC FAR WEST]

Even at the start of the 20th century,
Los Angeles had a reputation for being strange
and exotic - a real attraction for adventurous travelers
from the East and Midwest. In addition to
showcasing mansions, beach-front hotels and public
buildings, this viewbook offered an intriguing
look at some of the region's unusual flora and fauna.
Land developers also used the album
to cast the territory in a positive light and
counter its reputation for being a
waterless, desert plain.

C ompletion of the transcontinental railroad in 1869 and celebration of the United States Centennial in 1876 boosted American tourism in the late 19th century and stimulated national pride. Travelers clamored for souvenir pictures of places they had visited, and proud Americans sought mementos of historic national achievements to display in their parlors.

With halftone printing and hand-held cameras yet to be introduced, U.S. publishers collaborated with printers in Germany to convert photographs or drawings into stone lithographic reproductions. Between 1870 and 1915, this roundabout method resulted in thousands of souvenir albums featuring American landmarks, scenic views and national events. Competition to produce these miniature albums – typically $3\frac{1}{2}$ x 4 inches to $6\frac{1}{4}$ x $9\frac{1}{2}$ inches in size – became so feverish in the 1880s that The American Bookmaker described this "summer resort printing" as a "war of the monotint booklet." Until recently scholars dismissed the value of these tiny albums, but today researchers recognize their documentary importance, and museums and libraries are beginning to collect and catalog them. Fascinating not only for their historical content, these albums mark a transitional period in the development of photography, design and lithography.

[SEE THE WORLD BY RAIL]

Railways opened up the American frontier and made it
possible for common folks to see the continent in relative comfort.
Sold or given away at railroad depots, luggage shops
and stationers, souvenir albums catered to this new market by touting
the modern mode of transportation the traveler was likely
to enjoy and the scenic and cultural highlights - and sometimes
the major hotels - along the route.

The pictures in souvenir albums were not photographs; they were redrawn from photographs onto stone. Printers used a multi-pass process to achieve a range of tones. When varnished, the pictures looked like photographs.

While pictures in souvenir albums were created
to present contemporary views of local landmarks and industries,
today they provide scholars with realistic "snapshots"
of daily life in an earlier era. This 19th-century scene
of the Port of New Orleans captures a time when
cotton was still king and steamboats rested in the harbor before
heading back up the Mississippi River.

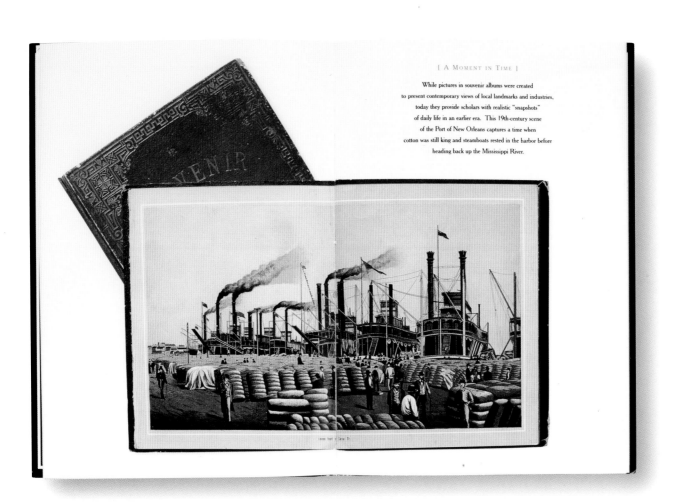

[PATRIOTIC PRIDE]

The Spanish-American War of 1889 aroused nationalist fervor
in the United States, and symbols of American patriotism became a favorite

and frequent theme in souvenir albums. This gallery of U.S. Presidents –
right up to Benjamin Harrison in 1889– depicts America's champions of freedom.

Published primarily in the 1880s, souvenir albums brought the wonders of the world to people who often had never ventured more than 50 miles from home. Through the marvel [...] tour the newly built Statue [...] paper. They could see Ni[...] War battlegrounds, distan[...] may have only been describ[...] 25 cents to $1.50, these m[...] of documentary reality una[...]

Like souvenir [...] gave rise to them survived [...] – quickly disappearing after 1895 with the introduction of photomechanical processes that allowed photographs to be reproduced directly instead of being redrawn.

For the most part, lithographic miniatures were printed on one side on a single long sheet of paper, then folded accordion-style, and pasted onto the inside front of a [...] mimic [...] or three languages.

A predecessor to today's travel postcards, souvenir albums had a much greater impact on the public at large, exposing them to sights that they had only tried to imagine.

[MIDWINTER EXPOSITION]

Souvenir albums were mass produced for international expositions
and world fairs, which attracted hordes of tourists at the turn of the century.
Every album featured a bird's eye view (following page). Because
the picture was made by redrawing photographic images onto printing stones,
the lithographic artist could easily eliminate unsightly things and
enlarge people in scale and pose them as he pleased. In the Victorian style,
naturalistic flowers bordered the picture.

To give readers an actual sense of a real souvenir album, Kit Hinrichs reproduced one on the Statue of Liberty at 3¼-by-4¼-inch size and had it stitched into the center of the book. Like the original, it presented all the images in an accordion fold.

Panoramic aerials of towns and industrial complexes were a favorite point of view in souvenir albums. Photographed in segments from a hot-air balloon or high hill and pieced together, the photographic original was redrawn into a single image, with the artist taking stylistic liberties to artfully arrange ships and clean up the facades of buildings.

MARKET & THIRD STREET

CLIFF HOUSE & SEAL ROCKS

PALACE HOTEL

CALIFORNIA & SANSOME STREET

FORT POINT & GOLDEN GATE

U.S. FORT, ALCATRAZ ISLAND

No. 3: **Brushes and Brooms**

Back Story

Pentagram's friendship
with collector Lou P. Klein
came about somewhat
circuitously, when Klein
came to London from
America to replace designer
Bob Gill at an advertising
agency named Hobson. Gill
had joined Alan Fletcher
and Colin Forbes to become
Fletcher/Forbes/Gill
(predecessor to Pentagram).
Over the years, the London
partners were fascinated by
the countless things that
Klein collected, particularly
his brushes and brooms.
Today the Louis P. Klein
Broom and Brush Museum
in Arcola, Illinois, is the
repository for what is
claimed to be the largest
collection of antique
brooms and brushes in
the United States.

A collection often starts without the collector's awareness that it is becoming one. Such was the case for American designer Lou P. Klein, who served as the head of graphic design at London's Royal College of Art. Klein originally bought a broom to clean his workshop, but found it so beautiful that he couldn't bring himself to use it on a dirty floor. So, he went out to get another one—only to find it was even more interesting than the first. Initially, Klein admits, he set a budget of 25p per brush, finding even cheaper ones in junk shops. One day, however, he realized that he had become "truly bitten" and that "price became practically no object"—he went up to 50p.

Klein's fascination with brushes turned into an obsession and a desire to "collect every damn brush in the world . . . even the ugly brush became nice . . . nice and ugly." He ran an ad in *Exchange & Mart*, hoping to locate some rare brushes he coveted, and among the stall holders in the Portobello Road market near his home, he became known as "the guy who collects brushes." No matter. Klein had become a brush connoisseur, able to distinguish nuances that eluded the less sophisticated viewer of brushes.

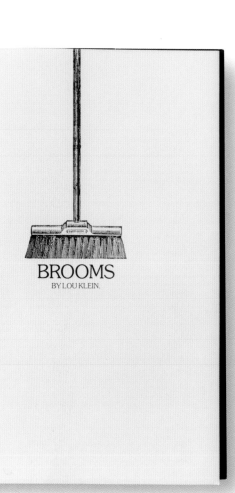

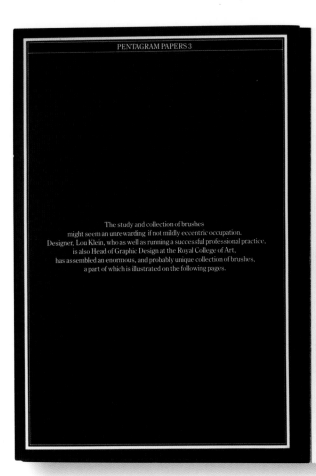

Lou P. Klein's interest grew out of an aesthetic appreciation for the design of these tools, but the larger his collection grew, the more interest he took in learning about the materials from which each was made and the history of how some were used.

Klein appreciated novelty brushes and brooms as well as the differences in materials and shapes. He pronounced Japanese brushes "masterpieces" and lauded the "timeless sculptural and tactile" qualities of brushes from Africa, Asia, and the Pacific.

No. 6: **Would You Care to Make a Contribution?**

Back Story

What captured partner John McConnell's interest in producing a Pentagram Paper on charity ephemera was the knowledge that collector Brian Love brought to the subject. "We don't just want pictures," McConnell says. "We try to find people who are authorities on the subject." In addition to owning more than 20,000 charity flags and 180 different donation boxes, Love had written several articles on printed ephemera and the book *Play the Game,* which describes board games from the eighteenth century to the early twentieth century.

British artist and designer Brian Love's collection of charity ephemera reveals a historical look at fund-raising for worthy causes over the past several centuries. Included among the thousands of items in Love's collection are amusing ploys used by fund-raisers to attract a shilling or two.

Love points out that practically every public social service in operation in England today started as some form of voluntary organization. Although the Poor Law Act passed by the British Parliament in 1601 deemed it the duty of each parish to provide for the sick, needy, and homeless, in reality, it was benevolent English citizens who continued to shoulder a large share of the burden.

Over the centuries, thousands of charitable societies have emerged, dedicating themselves to social needs and scientific, medical, and cultural causes as well as obscure interests such as a still-active trust founded in 1392 to maintain a stone bridge over the River Medway.

Love's collection of paper ephemera and donation boxes tells a tale of the charitable causes that the British have championed over the years.

A subscription card for the Ragged School Union.

The Welfare State owes a great debt to the English men and women, past and present, who have pointed out various social needs and then helped to create organisations to meet those needs. Practically every public Social Service in operation today started like this, as some form of voluntary organisation.

The first Parliamentary attempt to provide for the poor of England was the Poor Law Act of 1601. This laid upon each Parish the duty of providing from the rates for the sick, needy and homeless; thus establishing the principle that the care of such people should be part of the social structure. However, for the next 200 years or so the main burden was borne by benevolent citizens. To give or leave something to the poor of the community came to be expected of any prosperous Englishman and almshouses, hospitals and schools were founded throughout the country, on an astonishing scale.

The major instrument of Tudor Stuart philanthropy was the Charitable Trust, a gift or bequest made in perpetuity for charitable purposes. (The Poor Law included in its list of charitable objectives "the support of young handicraftsmen or decayed persons" and "the marriage of poor maids".) During the first three decades of the seventeenth century, thousands of pounds were subscribed, in charitable trusts, principally from the merchant community.

In the eighteenth century the wealthy few continued to make donations, and during the early part of the century over fifty voluntary hospitals were founded from private funds. Among these were the "Hospital for Poor French Protestants and Their Descendants Residing in Great Britain", known as the French Hospital, which was established in 1718, in South Hackney, London. Numerous private schools were also started; but no provision was made for even elementary instruction of children of the labouring classes. It was not until 1802 that the first steps were taken towards compulsory education.

The distinctive new idea in the nineteenth century was the Charitable Society. Throughout the century such organisations multiplied at a fantastic rate, dedicating themselves to Scientific, Medical and Cultural causes, and few social needs failed to be represented by their special agencies.

There were of course silly as well as sensible causes, with both struggling and well-established institutions, ranging from The Aborigines Protection Society (1836) and The Ragged School Union (1844) to The Salvation Army and The National Children's Home in the 1860's. Their numbers were considerable and their activities so overlapping that their policies often came under criticism from the Church and legal authorities.

From 1815 to 1850, prolonged investigations were made into the condition of charities, leading to the Charitable Trusts Act of 1853 and the formation of the Board of Charity Commissioners for England and Wales. Since this time, the Charity Commissioners, now in London's Haymarket, have maintained a register of charities; a record of the hopes, good deeds and ambitions not only of the major national charities, but also of thousands of small ones, representing almost as many different needs.

The popular idea that there may be vast sums of money lying unused in some forgotten bank account from the estate of an ancient charity is far from the truth. Analysis of the Charity Register indicates that well over half of all charities have a yearly income of less than £100, including about 23%, which receive less than £5 per year*. Many of these charities are receiving a tiny sum each year from an investment made several centuries ago, since a Charitable Trust is exempt from the legal rule against perpetuities, and may be created to have effect for ever.

Some of these ancient charities, however, are by no means obsolescent. The Rochester Bridge Trust was founded in about 1392 by Sir John de Cobbam and Sir Robert de Knolles. The charity's primary objective was maintenance of the stone bridge over the River Medway, which they had built to replace the wooden original. Endowments of the Trust include land and securities yielding a gross annual income of about £200,000 – still enough to maintain the dual carriageway bridges which cross the river today.

Trends in the type of charities being registered today reflect the changing outlook and needs of society. The report of the Charity Commissioners, 1976, states that "the largest class of new charities legalised during 1976, representing 22%, of the total, covers social welfare and cultural purposes; village halls, recreation grounds, trusts for furtherance of education in the arts, and the environmental trusts". Large numbers of today's new charities are concerned with such areas as drug addiction, one parent families and family planning; paving the way for tomorrow's Social Services.

Profits from the sale of this annual went to the Poppy Day Fund of the British Legion.

*J P Gallagher: "The Price of Charity"

COLLECTING FOR THE BIG CHARITIES

A collection envelope for Christian Aid week. Hundreds of these were distributed in the Metropolitan area.

House to house collection envelope celebrating the Salvation Army's centenary in 1929.

When the Spastics Society ran short of human flag sellers in 1970, students at the Hornsey College of Art constructed Bartholomew Proton X 12, with flashing lights and a revolving head, as a substitute.

A 1977 Oxfam campaign appealed for pre-decimal coins. Among the 100,000 coins received were many collectors' items, including this sixpence from the reign of Elizabeth I, dated 1562.

Lifeboat Saturday was the idea of Sir Charles Macara, a Lancashire businessman, and was first held in Salford, Manchester, in October 1891. There was a procession of lifeboats, three bands and Fire and Ambulance detachments. Money was thrown from windows and tops of trams, and more than £600 was collected.

A schoolboy collecting on Lifeboat Saturday, 20 May 1907, at Southend-on-Sea.

One of the twenty thousand people who walked up to 30 miles in aid of Oxfam on 13 July 1969. It was Britain's biggest-ever charity walk. Walkers were sponsored by the mile, and between them raised over £60,000.

The S.S. Iolé was one of eleven vessels that, in the 1880's comprised the fund raising "Salvation Navy", an erstwhile maritime extension of the Salvation Army. In 1886 the Iolé broke up on a sandbank in the mouth of the Humber, the crew barely escaping with their lives.

A look at Brian Love's charity-box collection proves that fund-raising devices have changed little over the centuries. There were charity events, raffles, fund-raising sales, commercial tie-ins, poster campaigns, and walkathons.

CHILDREN

Children selling firewood from the back of a donkey cart, in aid of the National Children's Home in 1870. The background is in fact a painted backdrop.

These 'before' and 'after' photographs were published in 1876 and sold in aid of Dr Barnado's. Although the models were genuine Barnado's boys, Barnado was later sued for having the 'before' pictures posed.

A Christmas card sold on behalf of the Ragged School Union in 1891. Like many charities of the time, the Ragged School Union chose a name for itself that made a strong appeal to the Victorian taste for mawkish sentimentality.

A 1977 appeal to build a children's home in Leicester. Every Heinz label saved was worth 1p. £100,000 was raised.

A Barnado's metal transfer printed collection box of the 1890's.

These sachets were sold in aid of soldiers' comforts during World War I, by children at St George's Roman Catholic School.

This issue of seals, used on letters and parcels, was officially exempted from Purchase Tax. Proceeds were divided equally between the Propaganda and Spitfire Funds.

Mr Lee, the proprietor of the Crown Inn, Hastings, decided to collect money to provide cigarettes for the troops in World War II. He asked customers to dip coins into their beer and stick them to the mirror, and he is shown here placing the last coin on the glass.

A disc leaflet dropped by a flying circus aeroplane over Trafalgar Square in 1918, advertising the Victory Loan.

An invitation from Margate taxi drivers to a Welcome Home Banquet given for sailors and soldiers who had done their bit in World War I.

This outsize bullet had a number of different slots for collecting anything from halfpenny to half crown contributions to the Silver Bullet Fund. It was inaugurated by Miss Ursula Bloom in October 1940 with three halfpence contributed by Lord Nuffield.

An aerial leaflet dropped over Luton in 1941 by the RAF, as part of the effort to raise half a million pounds during Watford War Weapons Week. It was "Issued in spite of Hitler, by the Displays and Stunts Sub-Committee".

Smiling 1940 girls accept an invitation to "Help sink the U-boat". A shilling's worth of pennies donated to the Woollen Fund for Comforts for Sailors, and placed in the conning-tower, achieved the grisly objective by sinking this model.

Jack the monkey spent many months with troops in France. Having had a toe shot away, and been a victim of a German gas attack he retired to Clifton Zoo, where he helped to collect money for his regiment's cigarette fund.

More prevalent a century ago than today was the use of collection boxes. This Pentagram Paper displayed some of the boxes Love owned in a double-gatefold spread (see next page), which was the only part of the book printed in color.

R.S.P.C.A.
PLEASE HELP
THANK YOU
PROVIDES FREE VETERINARY TREATMENT BY QUALIFIED VETERINARY SURGEONS FOR THE SICK AND INJURED ANIMALS OF THE POOR.
CONGREGATIONAL CHURCH,
LEYTONSTONE.
BUILDING FUND
S P G
Medical Missions.
THE SALVATION ARMY
GRACE BEFORE MEAT BOX
WAIFS & STRAYS
WAR EMERGENCY.
OUR WORK MUST GO ON
5,000 CHILDREN NOW UNDER OUR CARE
THE "WAIFS AND STRAYS"
CMS
RAF
1347

No. 22: **Architectural Toys**

Back Story

For years, architect and partner James Biber watched his old friend, New York caterer Paul Neuman, grow his collection of architectural toys from a few novelty pieces to one of the most extensive in the nation. In Biber, Neuman found an appreciative cohort who enjoyed surveying the latest acquisitions and playing with the toys. Explaining his own fascination, Biber says, "They combine, in deceptive simplicity and harmony, all the disciplines, the vision, and the talent a designer may hope for. They are at once graphics and architecture, product and package, model and reality." Since there was virtually nothing written about architectural toys, Biber felt that Neuman's collection was the perfect topic for a Pentagram Paper, and he collaborated with partner Paula Scher in designing the book.

Architectural toys—made of wood, paper, clay, stone, and other materials—have been around for centuries. More than merely appealing to a child's desire to stack and build, these toys expose children to the concept of architecture and urban environments. They reveal visual differences in public buildings such as post offices and banks. Some invite users to arrange whole villages to their liking. They force contemplation of structural shapes, landmark features, and cultural styles, and show architectural details and spatial relationships between buildings.

Architectural toys evolved over the decades, from stacked blocks and houses of cards with special notches for easy assembly to a variety of shaped wooden and simulated stone blocks, and finally to analogues of steel-frame construction. Intended as instructional devices, they allowed a child to control and understand architecture and context. Until the age of plastics, the toys were usually made of the materials they represented and often dealt with real architectural issues: form, style, detail, material, and construction. Hence, these toys serve as the perfect primer on architecture.

DONATIONS

ESTABLISHMENT.
Dreadnought Hospital Greenwich, 225 beds
Victoria & Albert Docks Hospital, 50 beds
Dispensary — East India Dock Road E.
Dispensary — Gravesend

POSTAL ADDRESS
GREENWICH, S.E.
BANKERS
WILLIAMS, D & Co
LONDON & COUNTY BANK
GREENWICH BRANCH

MENS HOSPITAL SOCIETY

BY VOLUNTARY CONTRIBUTIONS

SAILORS OF CHINA

Primitive Methodist
AFRICAN MISSIONS
THE FAMILY OFFERINGS
TO CHRIST FOR AFRICA

HELP
TO HELP THEMSELVES

GRACE MEAD
PLEASE STAND THIS
BOX ON YOUR
DINNER TABLE

LONDON
CHEST
HOSPITAL

MILK — MILK
GALLONS USED
ANNUALLY
Please
for Health

RUANDA
MISSION

CMS

CHILDREN AND THE INFIRM

THE BRIDGE
FROM HOME TO THE FIELD
GIFT

Russian
Monastery,
hand painted
and gilded
wood,
Russian, 1850

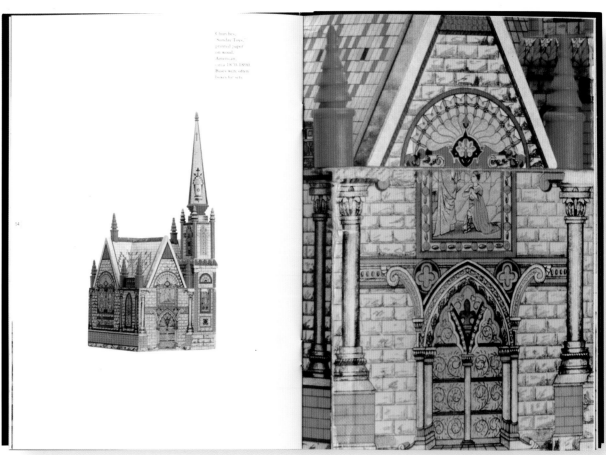

Churches,
Sunday Toys,
printed paper
on wood,
American,
circa 1870-1890.
Boxes were often
homes for sets.

Architectural toys have been created by cultures around the world for centuries. Made of hand-painted wood or stone, early toys let children reconstruct an entire village and study architectural details close up.

Village,
hand painted
wood, American,
circa 1920

FOLLOWING PAGE:

LEFT:
Summer Colony Set,
packed in box, painted
wood, German,
circa 1880

RIGHT:
Stone Blocks,
German, 1913

The architectural style of different periods in history and building landmarks that were important to a village or metropolis are evident in these toys. For some complex toy sets, manufacturers included a plan for how to pack the pieces in a box (bottom left).

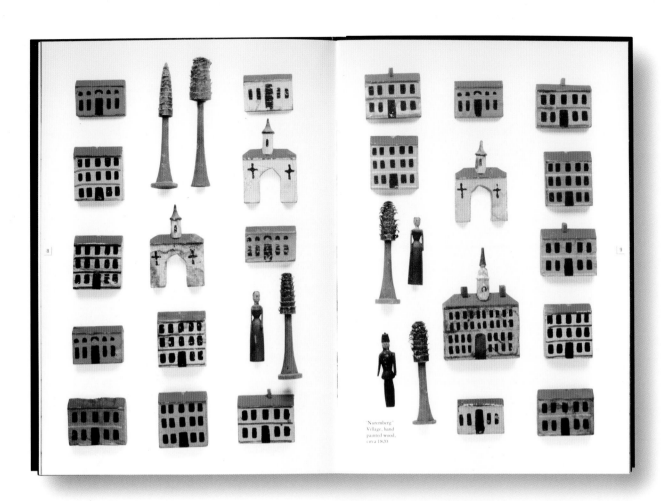

'Nuremberg'
Village, hand
painted wood,
circa 1820

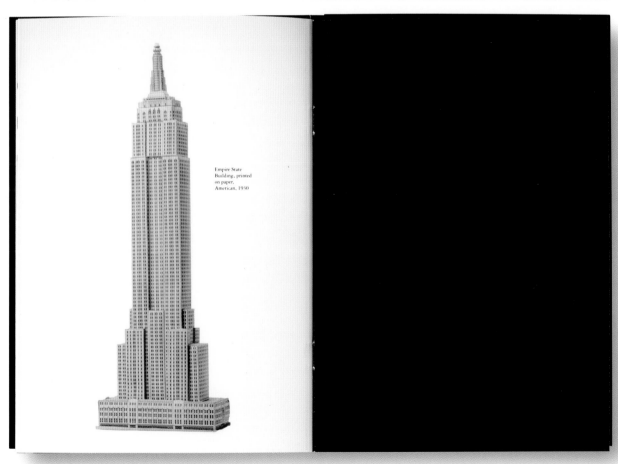

Empire State
Building, printed
on paper,
American, 1930

Retrospection

Hindsight not only improves vision, it enhances appreciation. It allows for looking beyond the original purpose and, from the leisurely perspective afforded by the passage of time, seeing things in a broader context. Perhaps only after the slide rule has lost its utility can one view it as an object of beauty. So, too, can we reflect on the heroism of unsung printers who ran the underground presses during the Nazi occupation of France. Or reconsider the lights of the Savoy hotel, which were celebrated at the time because they heralded the exciting age of electricity, not a new decorative style. Time erases memories of how it was, where it began, why it had to happen that way. Like unearthing keepsakes in an attic, reminders of our past are cause for introspection and sometimes a release from our myopic view of the world.

No. 13: **Imprimeries Clandestines**

Back Story

Knowing that London-based art director David King had the largest Russian graphics collection in the Western world, partner John McConnell originally suggested that he write an article on El Lissitzky for a Pentagram Paper. King replied he had something better in mind. While browsing a second-hand bookstore in Paris, King had discovered a 1945 pamphlet, *Le Point*, that provided first-person accounts written by people who worked for an underground publishing house in Nazi-occupied Paris. Pentagram had the forgotten pamphlet translated into English and reprinted it as a Pentagram Paper.

Under the censorious forces of the grim and ruthless Nazi occupation, French writers and printers went underground and secretly formed the publishing house, *Les Éditions de Minuit.* Although some were arrested and tortured, shot, hung, or sent to the death camps, the publishers refused to cease their clandestine activities. *Le Point,* itself published clandestinely in 1945, provides first-person accounts of those who defiantly risked all in order to ensure the ongoing production of fine and even lavish work that lived up to the highest French standards of literature and printing.

Every step of the process was fraught with danger, from the entrusting of the manuscripts by the writers, poets, and critics to the secret distribution of the books to those who hungered to keep intellectual thought alive. Manuscripts were sometimes smuggled in cargos of fruit. The text was set in a home on a portable linotype, with the heavy metal type carried to the secret printer on foot or bike. As soon as the copy was printed, the type was destroyed. For their own safety, everyone worked in anonymity, not knowing who their compatriots were. In spite of the peril, *Les Éditions de Minuit* published twenty-five volumes during the Nazi occupation. Still, more than a dozen contributors died as they dedicated themselves to the cause.

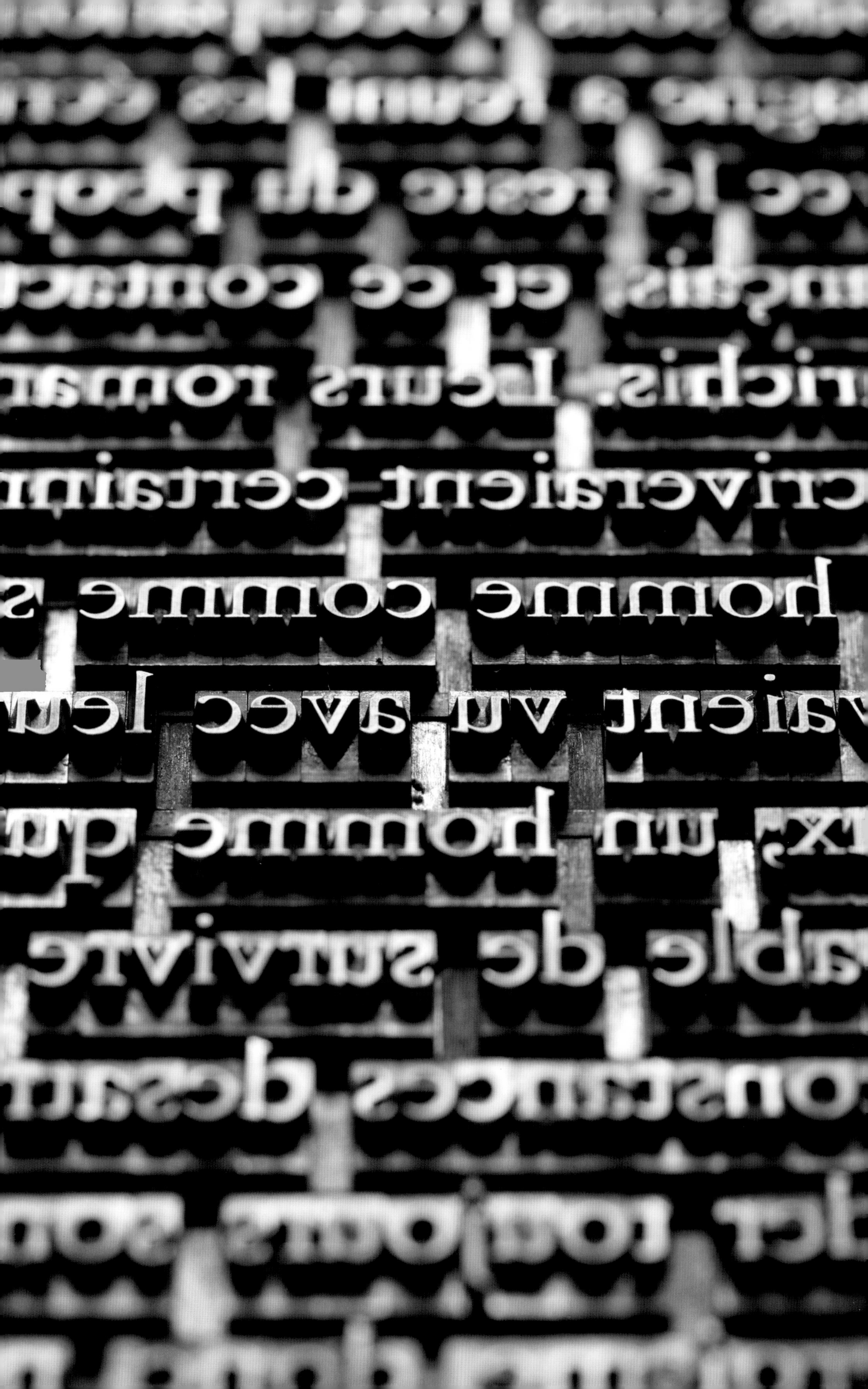

homme comme s

vaient vu avec leu

x, un homme q

ble de survivre

Under the censorious forces of the grim and ruthless Nazi occupation, French printers went underground to preserve their liberty. This edition of *Le Point*, itself a clandestine publication, was discovered recently by English designer David King in a Parisian second-hand bookshop. It is a tribute to the work of the underground presses and the power of their tenacious commitment to freedom of expression.

UNDERGROUND
PRESSES

XXXI

MARCH 1945

LE POINT
AN ARTS AND LITERARY REVIEW
PUBLISHED EVERY TWO MONTHS
SIXTH YEAR
LANZAC, PAR SOUILLAC (LOT)

C. Ebener (quartier de la République), an escaped prisoner who printed underground newspapers, leaflets and pamphlets by night and took part in the fighting at place de la République during the liberation of Paris.

While memories were fresh, members of the French underground press told their personal stories for a 1945 edition of *Le Point*.

VERCORS

About Necessary Chances

As with all human enterprises, there was a good deal of chance involved in the birth of Les Editions de Minuit – but 'chance' is after all only our way of summing up a multiplicity of causes which we do not know how to synthesize or reduce to an intelligible number. For where chance is confused with necessity and necessity is served by chance (even if we cannot dissolve the obvious bonds), our reason has to yield in the presence of a mysterious will.

We know what the necessity was: to let France express her essential spirit and find in secrecy the material means to make this expression possible. The underground press could not readily provide these means. Did France find them in Les Editions de Minuit? It seems reasonable to doubt it. The principal means at the disposal of thought were the newspapers and, for the most important items, reviews. These are the ordinary means of fulfilling the demands of expression, but in difficult times expression is generally obliged to make do with any means at its disposal. It is plausible to suggest that, in the absence of a clandestine book publisher, few works were conceived which would have exceeded the dimensions of the underground newspaper or

10

A RARE COPY OF 'LE SILENCE DE LA MER' IN THE EDITION PRINTED BY CLAUDE OUDEVILLE.

July 1942. In the meantime Jacques Decour and Georges Politzer had been shot as hostages, remaining silent despite all that torture and their executioners' hatred could do to them. Now Claude Morgan still had to find a way of contacting Jean Paulhan, whom he did not know, just as he no longer knew the identities of his friends on the Committee. In the interim, since he was alone, he himself assumed responsibility for the appearance of *Les Lettres Françaises*.

Other intellectuals were forming committees and getting ready to publish underground newspapers modelled on *L'Université Libre*. Notable examples were the Front National du Palais, which was soon distributing its own *Le Palais Libre*, in which traitors were later so boldly unmasked, and the admirable *Témoignage Chrétien* which, under the leadership of Father Maydieu, a founder member of the National Committee of Writers, campaigned so bravely and effectively, especially among young Catholics.

The first number of *Les Lettres Françaises*, duplicated by roneo, appeared on 20 September 1940, the anniversary of Valmy. When the novelist Edith Thomas returned to Paris, she put Claude Morgan in touch with Jean Paulhan and Jacques Debû-Bridel, and it is thanks to her that the National Committee of Writers was eventually reconstituted. It was clear that there were traitors to be dealt with, and the first issues undertook this 'public health' work with passionate commitment. Yet in so far as this activity was negative, it would soon no longer do. As clearly as circumstances would permit, the magazine's message had to reach all those of us whose dogged patriotism and courage never wavered. It had to write about the sufferings and battling courage of the French people. It had to extol the heroes. It had to call for a national uprising.

Meanwhile the National Committee of Writers was gaining in importance, its ranks gradually swelled by writers, poets and critics. One of the first to join the little Committee was the excellent Eluard, whose conscientiousness, compassion and courage are well known. He was actively involved in editing and distributing *Les Lettres Françaises*, as well as contributing his best poems. He was also an adviser to Les Editions de Minuit, and he planned and published *L'Honneur des Poètes* with Jean Lescure of the review *Messages*. Again with Jean Lescure he saw through the successful publication of *Domaine Français*, which was produced in Switzerland with the collaboration of almost all French writers and which included contributions from Jacques Decour and Saint-Pol-Roux, both murdered by the barbarous Nazis. Finally, to round off this too brief summary of his astounding activities, in the last stage of the Occupation, he launched an underground poetry magazine. Its title affirmed the indestructibility of poetry, which, like the phoenix, is always reborn from

26

PONTREMOLI (CENTRE), A PAINTER WHO PUT ASIDE HIS BRUSHES TO SET UP A SMALL PRINTING PRESS IN HIS HOME. WORKS FOR THE MLN WITH HIS WIFE AND ANOTHER PAINTER, PHILIBERT (QUARTIER DE L'OPÉRA).

CLAUDE OUDEVILLE, PRINTER OF VISITING CARDS AND INVITATIONS AND COMPOSITOR OF 'LE SILENCE DE LA MER'.

Le Silence de la mer had had a close shave and now found itself homeless. But why not publish it as a book? Vercors knew a printer who would take the risk, and the printed sheets could be brought to my house near the Trocadéro for sewing. We would organize a distribution network and, if the venture was successful, why should we not continue to publish books, printed, sewn and distributed in secret, forging a chain between everyone who thought as we did and beyond German control? In this way Les Editions de Minuit was founded. It must have been born under a lucky star for, in the teeth of all opposition, it survived until August 1944 with all sails unfurled and a cargo of twenty-five books published in the space of two and a half years.

I am often asked how we funded Les Editions de Minuit. It has even been said, and written, that the quality and elegance of our little books could scarcely have been achieved without financial support from the Germans. The truth is very simple. We had started with a donation of 3,000 francs from a well-wisher; a second donation of 5,000 francs after the publication of the first book made it possible to produce the second volume. We began to be known in Resistance circles and could easily have accepted the money that was offered by more than one group, but we preferred to work independently. We would cover our expenses by selling part of every edition to whoever could buy our books, and so we could afford to give the rest away. When we were able to increase the print run, our income exceeded our costs; overall, far from taking money from the Resistance, we made a profit of more than 300,000 francs, which was shared, via the National Committee of Writers, among the families of partisan printers who had died doing clandestine work. You have to admit that 'German money' never served a nobler cause!

Le Silence de la mer was published in February 1942 in an edition of only 350 copies, folded and sewn at my place and bound by Vercors himself on my kitchen table. Many of these volumes have since been lost or destroyed, but, thanks to the enthusiastic readers who circulated it under wraps and the intrepid resisters who took it to London, this little book was read by millions around the world even before we decided to print a second edition.

But one man never read it. Jacques Decour, who was responsible for all the underground literature in Paris, was arrested on the very day that *Le Silence* was printed. He was shot by the Germans three months later, in May 1942. He is gone, but his work remains; the example he set has been followed. The school where he taught now bears his name, and we have published a booklet about him and his work.

15

CHARLES PRONET (ALIAS BRUNET), ENGRAVING, IN FULL VIEW OF THE PUBLIC, FRANCIQUES AND EAGLES ON SEALS FOR USE ON FORGED DOCUMENTS. HE KEPT HIS 'WORK IN PROGRESS' IN A HOLLOW BEAM.

ENGRAVING A FRANCISQUE

The photographs in this Pentagram Paper were provided by the widow of Robert Doisneau, who, while working for the French Resistance during World War II, shot secret photographs of the printers at work.

Honouring our Fellow Printers

The Germans were quite right to burn books, and Victor Hugo, who was not as stupid as some traitors wanted us to believe, was quite right to say that books are weapons and that words can kill. Let us honour the clandestine printing industry which flourished during our slavery! And let us honour our fellow printers who worked unpaid through the nights and rebuked us when we offered them something for their efforts. 'Rubbish!' they said. 'This is our way of fighting!' Everyone has his job to do, and the Germans were doing theirs in hunting down clandestine publications and, when these escaped their clutches, raiding legitimate bookshops. Books can always be seized, even if the act is legal only in the eyes of an inquisitor or some forgotten parliament. For everything monstrous, barbarous, inane and intolerable that thrived in the darkness of history has been made real, present, urgent, necessary and ineluctable by the Germans. So they were doing their job when they used every means at their disposal to broadcast their sadistic pornography through the writings of the late Drieu and his wretched lackeys (where did they come from? What spawned them?). The 'business of literature' – to borrow a brilliant and very Parisian editorial expression – continued beneath the flood of filth which looked like printed words, collected in what seemed to be articles, newspapers and books. The *true* literary business, the real thing, was the leaflets, books, poems, reviews, editorial meetings and boys who got themselves arrested by going back to a cellar to correct a misprint or by checking a suitcase out of a railway station.

A general rule: don't move if you trip over a barrier in the Métro tunnel because there will be a cop just behind you, watching you closely, ready to collar you. Isn't that so, Etienne? (On that particular day Etienne, who carried suitcases around every day, was the first suspect to insist that his case contained no *Cahiers de la Libération*.) Doubtless this was not much to get arrested or even to risk arrest for, but this 'not much' made the brutes tremble with fear. You also have to believe that this little thing was something and must see that our Resistance printers were worthy successors to the printers of the 'Trois Glorieuses' and the '48, who melted their lead for bullets. Fly, little winged character, flaming spirit, insolent saboteur!

Even the mysterious Jean Paulhan loved to be at the heart of these laboratories-cum-arsenals, and he made this moving comment about them: 'It is less than a bee sting on the terrible hand that traps us, but if the bees didn't sting, there would be no more bees.' The supreme art of the word, written and reproduced in the humblest, roughest forms, has hurled its spear.

It started with typing on scraps of paper. This same Jean Paulhan had to face the Gestapo on account of a roneoed newspaper – a Resistance of our own – about the Musée de l'Homme affair. We had drafted it with Claude Avelin in the very flat (it belonged to dear Martin-Chauffiers) where Emmanuel d'Astier was hunted down and captured two years later, never to return.

But the printers hurried to the rescue. In the bitter autumn of 1940 we in Paris were already admiring the elegant, perfect typography and design of *Pantagruel* with much interest and not without envy. The provincial and Parisian printers did their desperate duty, and some of them were famous names in the trade: art and de luxe printers, master printers in whose workrooms, smelling of ink, we rediscovered the delights of layout, proof correction and minute technical discussion.

I want to end my tribute to the noblest of trades by recollecting two of its martyrs: the Lion brothers of Toulouse who, with splendidly southern largesse, gaiety and recklessness, made their workrooms the regional centre for all underground printing. Forged documents as well as pamphlets and newspapers came off their presses – in short, anything that put pressure on the enemy. Their impassioned courage was defeated by the Gestapo, by deportation to Germany and, finally, by the death ovens. My friends, you, as French printers, keep alive the memory of the Lion brothers, those heroes of free expression. They, and so many of your own comrades, died so that *this* could kill *that*.

France is now utterly destitute, and the printers, short as they are of materials and paper and with so many gaps in their ranks, cannot restore their finest traditions of craftsmanship overnight. Here, as everywhere else, everything has to be rebuilt slowly and patiently; we are beginning at the bottom. Or rather, here as everywhere else, we are beginning with a humble, fertile and glorious commitment – that of faith. Every element and principle has been called in question: we have returned to the essential why and wherefore of each action and gesture, each choice of character and its typeface, each word and its spirit. Our beautiful, humane trade has survived its ordeal of darkness and blood.

Jean Cassou

4
5

---

militia, Elsa Triolet's and Georges Sadoul's reports on the Resistance fighters, a story by Andrée Viollis, selections from Péguy by André Rousseaux (which were eventually published by Les Editions de Minuit), etc.

At the beginning of 1944 the Gestapo's vigilance was making printing more difficult. The presses in Lyon, Toulouse and Saint-Flour fell one after another, and *Les Etoiles*, which had been printing throughout the year and publishing regularly once a month, was now appearing very late and coming off a press in Valence.

Problems with transport also increased. The Bibliothèque Française and *Les Etoiles* were using a complicated mode of distribution. Three couriers travelled the length and breadth of southern France with heavy suitcases full of pamphlets, leaflets and the little books from Les Editions de Minuit which were looked after in the provinces by *Les Etoiles*. Regional distribution centres were established at Toulouse, Marseille, Nice, Toulon, Montpellier, Clermont-Ferrand, Limoges, Grenoble and Lyon, from where the publications were taken to the less important towns.

By April 1944 it was obvious that our confused transport system would soon jeopardize the efficiency of our distribution. The regional centres of *Les Etoiles* made arrangements to have their printing done locally. Toulouse was first to produce results, and three pamphlets were printed in time to be distributed throughout the Southern Zone: *Pathologie des prisons allemandes en France*, which was actual reportage by two imprisoned doctors; *Guide de l'infirmier du Maquis* and *Pathologie de la France malheureuse et asservie*, both by Professor Debré of the Academy of Medicine.

Marseille published Robert Lanzer's German anti-Hitler poems, intended for the Wehrmacht; a press at Romans produced, besides the newspaper *La Drôme en Armes*, Aragon's *Dix chansons interdites* and Elsa Triolet's *Yvette*. Montpellier reissued *Le Silence de la mer*, and Nice did the same for the review *Pensée et Action*. Finally, after setting up a clandestine press in Figeac (in circumstances which have been described elsewhere), the groups in the Lot brought out a regional edition of *Les Etoiles* called *Les Etoiles du Quercy*, with the help of Jean Cassou, André Chamson, Jean Lurçat, Jean Marcenac, René Huyghes, etc.

These clandestine activities did not cease with the liberation. *Les Etoiles du Quercy* is still in production as a literary review published in Cahors. Since 15 May 1945 *Les Etoiles* has been an important Parisian weekly, and the Bibliothèque Française is now responsible for a vast range of literary and artistic titles.

Georges Sadoul

36

THE ARTRA PRESS (PLACE D'ITALIE) PRINTED THE 'CAHIERS DU TÉMOIGNAGE CHRÉTIEN', THE SECOND AND THIRD EDITIONS OF GENERAL DE GAULLE'S COLLECTED SPEECHES, THE POSTERS CALLING PARISIANS TO MAN THE BARRICADES AND ANY WORK THAT NEEDED A LARGE PRINT RUN.

Doisneau became one of France's most famous photojournalists. In the early 1950s, he worked for *Vogue*.

No. 28: **Of Money and the Divine**

Back Story

As an editor of the *Looking Closer* books, which feature critical writings on graphic design published by Allworth Press, partner Michael Bierut came to know Tad Crawford, Allworth's president and publisher. Crawford had studied economics at Tufts University and graduated from Columbia Law School—two interests he combined in his writing of the book *The Secret Life of Money* (Putnam, 1994). Noting that electronic commerce was beginning to make coins and paper currency irrelevant, the Pentagram partners decided it was an ideal time to remind people of the divine origin of money.

While many speak of the evils of money and condemn those who worship it, the origin of money was divine, explains Tad Crawford in an essay adapted from his book, *The Secret Life of Money.*

"It is no accident that the word money comes from the Roman fertility goddess named Moneta and that a temple sacred to Moneta housed the Roman mint," Crawford posits. Money evolved as an aspect of fertility, when the riches of the hunt and the fields were offered back to the spirit world to ensure further renewal.

As societies increasingly dealt with outsiders, money was used to facilitate the circulation of commodities. The temples at Delphi issued their first silver coins, bearing the likeness of Olympian gods, to support trade through issuance of coinage. After Corinth built the first treasury in the early sixth century B.C., the most powerful city-states followed suit until twenty treasuries lined the Sacred Way that ran through the sanctuary and past the Temple of Apollo. The divine origins of money have been lost to consciousness, yet vestiges remain, even in the coins and bills of the United States that firmly pledge, "In God We Trust."

WE OFTEN hear condemnations of the worship of money. These critics—whether of a society driven by consumption, of the inordinate millions made by stock market manipulators, or of the crass ostentation of certain of the wealthy—miss a fundamental point. The reason that so many people worship money is because money, in its origins, was divine. It is no accident that the word money comes from the Roman fertility goddess named Moneta and that a temple sacred to Moneta housed the Roman mint.

If we simply complain of the evils of money, we miss the opportunity to explore its symbolic richness. Certainly the Bible does not condemn money, but warns: "The love of money is the root of all evils." Not money, but the love of money, is the root of evil. If we love money, we are likely to lose sight of its deeper significance. If we literalize money as our goal, we fail to see it as a symbol of life forces that could connect us more deeply to ourselves, our families, and our communities. So the evil that flows from an attachment to money is done not only to ourselves, but also to those we most hope to love. In a sense, money challenges us to learn what is truly worthy of our love. If we understand the origins of money, we can direct our love away from money as we develop the potentials that it symbolizes.

This essay will explore how, thousands of years ago, the divine origins of money were lost to sight, lost to consciousness. We are left only with the device of money and its practical applications in the world. Of its sources and first purposes, we know nothing. Yet the initial religious fervor that forged money remains within us. It animates us and gives money a mystical allure. Mystical because we are unaware that in our imaginal world the touch of money can be experienced as contact with the divine.

Hints and vestiges of money's divine origins are present on money today–in some cases quite visible, in other cases more hidden. The coins and bills of the United States firmly pledge "In God We Trust." This is remarkable in a country whose Constitution guarantees the separation of Church and State. If a school board required students in public school to say "In God We Trust" each morning, the board would transgress the First Amendment. But the Treasury, as required by federal law, must place the phrase "In God We Trust" on all coins and bills. Each day hundreds of millions of people hand this phrase back and forth when they exchange money.

To delve into the most ancient origins of money, we will look first at societies that had no money. Money did not suddenly appear, fully imagined and realized, in the world. Rather, it came gradually and in response to the evolution of human needs. To understand the origins of money, we must see how cycles of exchange came to connect both hunting and agricultural societies to their gods, and how money and markets evolved from these cycles of exchanges.

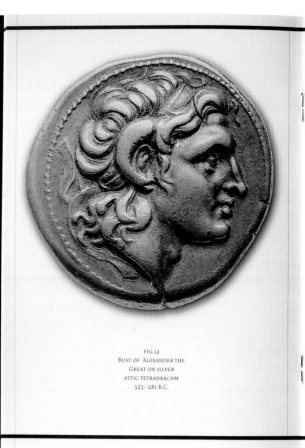

passed into their hands. Nonetheless, several centuries passed before the face of an actual person as opposed to that of a god or goddess appeared on a coin. This first portrait, that of Alexander the Great, dates to after Alexander's death. Alexander had declared himself a living god but was not officially deified until after his death. The use of his image reflected this deification and opened the way for living rulers to make godlike portrayals of themselves on coins.

ARCHITECTS FOR BANKS in the nineteenth and early twentieth century frequently turned for models to the ancient temples of Greece and Rome. The symbolic connection to the ancient treasuries aided the banks by implying a sacred imprimatur that would keep the money sound and the deposits safe. So many banks looked like temples, their magnificence imbued with the implicit power of the unseen divinities. Pillared facades, massive doors, and lofty interiors with vaulted ceilings all sought to inspire awe. To complete the sense that these buildings were large and impregnable vaults, the windows were often tiny. Even within the bank, the officers would be hidden from sight, with the give-and-take of money conducted by clerks in hushed voices.

On the reverse of the ten dollar bill is an engraving of the United States Treasury in Washington, D.C. Its wide steps leading heavenward, handsome pillars, and vast size all give credence to its sacred and inviolable role in our lives. The Treasury building, erected in 1836, is the third oldest building in Washington and is predated only by the White House and the Capitol.

The First Bank of the United States, designed by Samuel Blodget, Jr., and built in Philadelphia between 1795 and 1797, has a white marble

The Romans depicted the divine origin of money by using sacred symbols on coins and minting money in the temple of Moneta.

pilgrims would bring various forms of wealth. Protected by the sacred association with the temples, fairs developed for the purpose of exchange. In fact, the German word for Mass—*Messe*—also means fair.

One goal of pilgrims in the ancient world was to visit the famed oracle at Delphi in Greece. As early as 1400 B.C. a sanctuary of Gaia, goddess of the Earth and mother of the gods, existed on this mountainous site with its natural spring and panoramic views of Mount Kirfis and the Gorge of Pleistos running to the Gulf of Corinth. The myths tell of Apollo's killing of the female serpent that guarded the prophetic spring. Thus a male deity displaced Gaia, and from the eighth century onward Apollo, a culture-giving god of intellect, the arts, and prophecy, was worshiped there.

From all over the known world people came to consult the Delphic oracle for information from the gods. After paying a fee and sacrificing animals, the suppliant was brought into the inner shrine of the temple. Separated by a curtain from the priestess who sat on a sacred tripod and breathed intoxicating fumes rising from the rocks, the suppliant could hear her incomprehensible words and shouts. Male priests interpreted these utterances in the form of brief verses.

It's surprising when visiting Delphi today to find the ruins of treasuries beside the ruins of temples. Corinth built the first treasury at the beginning of the sixth century B.C. The most powerful city-states followed suit until twenty treasuries lined the Sacred Way that ran through the sanctuary and past the Temple of Apollo. The word treasury comes from the same root as the word thesaurus. It refers to a gathering of things, a repository. In addition to contributing to the support of the Temple of Apollo, the city-states would also dedicate riches to their treasuries. These elegant marble buildings filled

FIG.6
RECONSTRUCTION
OF THE TREASURY
OF THE ATHENIANS AT
DELPHI

FIG.7
THE TREASURY OF THE
ATHENIANS AT DELPHI
510 B.C.

hardly had a godless motive in removing the motto; rather, he felt the very mention of God in the motto to be a sacrilege. It is interesting that the suggested motto of "God, liberty, law," which says nothing about trusting, became "In God We Trust." The Secretary of the Treasury added the concept of trust. It almost seems that we are being asked to trust in God when, in fact, the government really wants us to trust in the currency and the government that issues it. This might explain Roosevelt's feelings. Also the currency was not trustworthy when the phrase first appeared, since the Civil War was financed by debt and inflation rather than taxes. In any event, President Eisenhower signed legislation in 1955 extending use of the motto to paper currency, and since 1957 "In God We Trust" has appeared on bills as well as coins.

The all-seeing eye did not appear on coins of the United States, as N.R. Watkinson wished, but we are all familiar with its presence today on our currency. The Great Seal of the United States, adopted in 1782, has both its front and reverse portrayed on the back of the one dollar bill. The reverse of the Great Seal shows an unfinished pyramid with the all-seeing eye contained in a triangle floating above it. This all-seeing eye is, of course, the eye of God contained in a triangle representing the Christian Trinity. Its presence on the Great Seal represents the desire of the Founding Fathers to have God oversee the continued building of the unfinished pyramid (nation) which they had begun. Not only was God's favor sought for the future, but His support for their efforts was unequivocally stated in the Latin phrase "annuit coeptis," which translates "He (God) has approved our undertakings." In fact, the color and motifs of United States paper money also arouse, at least unconsciously, associations with fertility cycles.

FIG.18
DETAIL OF THE
"ALL SEEING EYE"

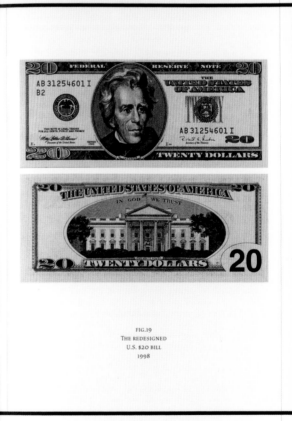

FIG.19
THE REDESIGNED
U.S. $20 BILL
1998

Divine protection is implied on United States currency, with the motto "In God We Trust" and the "all-seeing eye" of God on the top of a pyramid with the phrase *annuit coeptis*, or "He [God] has approved our undertaking."

No. 29: **Savoy Lights**

During the 1990s, the celebrated Savoy hotel in London underwent a major renovation, and partner John Rushworth was commissioned to create a new graphic identity for the historic building. While there, Rushworth kept noticing an amazing array of early-twentieth-century lighting fixtures throughout the building. "Despite all the various expansions and refurbishments to the hotel over the decades, the lighting stayed more or less the same," Rushworth says. The historic neon sign above the canopy entrance to the hotel had long been a London landmark, but an equally impressive part of the Savoy's identity was the lighting inside, Rushworth adds. Graham Vickers, author of *21st Century Hotel*, wrote the introduction to this Pentagram Paper, which features photography by Phil Sayer.

Ten years after Thomas Edison invented electric lighting, the Savoy in London's West End became the first fully electrified hotel when it opened for business in 1889. Richard D'Oyly Carte, impresario of Gilbert and Sullivan light operas, who built the Savoy as a companion to his adjoining theater, keenly understood how the right lighting could set the stage in a dramatic and alluring manner. In conceiving his hotel, he was determined to make everything the height of modernity and grandeur. Installing a power plant in the hotel basement to deliver electric lights to guests was audaciously extravagant. "Shaded electric lights everywhere at all hours of night and day . . . No gas or artificial light used. The light so shaded as to give no glare," proclaimed the Savoy's inaugural brochure. Another feature that the hotel boasted was the provision of seventy bathrooms—this at a time when the Savoy's nearest rival had only four bathrooms for five hundred guests. Such amenities made the Savoy the most chic hotel in London. Although the Savoy has subtly augmented lights over the years, it has appreciated and preserved its role as an electric pioneer, and maintained lighting that is emblematic of exquisite luxury and style.

As people began to travel for pleasure, a new class of luxury accommodation had developed, notably the French and Italian Riviera resort hotels which were designed for wealthy guests who might stay for an entire season. With good service a prerequisite, ambience became increasingly important. Soon distinctive luxury hotels began to appear in the cities too, with America offering glittering models such as The Palace in San Francisco. There developed an enthusiasm for providing the sort of theatrical flourishes that define a grand hotel as being as much a *mise en scène* as a provider of superior hospitality. The man behind The Savoy, Richard D'Oyly Carte, had originally built his theatre to satisfy the seemingly insatiable demand for the light operas of Gilbert & Sullivan; he clearly saw the companion hotel in related terms, with high standards of accommodation and dining accentuated by a shrewd sense of the dramatic. For example, the provision of 70 bathrooms was widely regarded at the time as an extravagant promotional gesture rather than a hygienic necessity. The Savoy's nearest contemporary rival had four bathrooms for 500 guests.

Working with youthful building architect C.B. Young, and interior architect T.E. Collcutt, D'Oyly Carte appears to have been the main creative force in his own hotel's design; the sudden almost magical availability of electric lighting must have seemed highly propitious to a man who took aesthetic advice from his ex-actress wife and who was to name each of his hotel's private dining rooms after a Gilbert & Sullivan opera.

Considered the height of luxury, the electric lights at the Savoy represented a daring modernity that the hotel strived to match in the stylishness of its décor. The Savoy quickly became the fashionable meeting place for the ultra-rich.

SAVOY LIGHTS

"The Savoy Hotel and Restaurant situated on the Victoria Embankment between Charing Cross and Waterloo Bridge (opposite Cleopatra's Needle) will open Tuesday next, 6th August. The perfection of luxury and comfort. Artistic furniture throughout. Electric light only everywhere, ready for use at all hours of day and night. No gas or artificial light used. The light so shaded as to give no glare."
The Times, 2 August 1889

In such terms did London's Savoy Hotel advertise its launch towards the end of the 19th century. Its companion building, The Savoy Theatre, which pre-dated the hotel by eight years on part of the same riverside site, had similarly made much of its early investment in illumination by electricity. However, while the theatre had to make do with a generator in a nearby shed, the hotel immediately installed its own power plant in the basement to deliver what it clearly saw as an exciting new attraction: electric light. *"Shaded electric lights everywhere at all hours of night and day"*, The Savoy's first brochure reaffirmed. *"No gas."*

The seductive imagery of light extended further into The Savoy's lexicon of luxury, as guests were encouraged to use the speaking tubes in their rooms to *"command anything from a cup of tea to a cocktail"* and were guaranteed with charming imprecision, that *"it will come up in the twinkling of an Embankment lamp"*.

The sheer novelty of the electric light may have been the primary reason for its high profile in the launching of The Savoy (after all Thomas Edison's 1879 invention was still a recent phenomenon), but it is perhaps no coincidence that the early adoption of electric lighting by theatres the world over had some relevance to the burgeoning role of the grand hotels of the late 19th century.

Left: Corridor from Room 516 looking West (n/s)

From the beginning, the Savoy used lighting in a theatrical manner to create an ambience of conviviality and warmth. While the hotel has undergone several renovations, its original lighting fixtures remain an elegant signature of the Savoy.

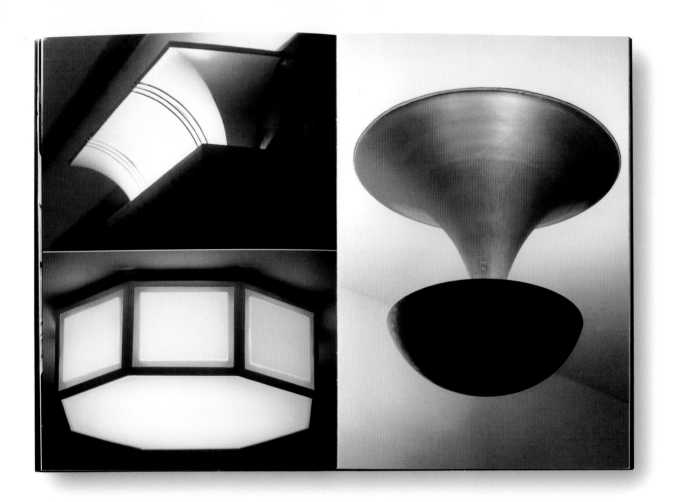

No. 15: **Through the Window**

Back Story

While sorting through boxes of books owned by his late father-in-law, partner Colin Forbes came across a number of early-twentieth-century travel guides. Among them was a pamphlet on England, which his father-in-law undoubtedly bought while he was a medical student in London prior to World War I. For British-born Forbes, the *Through the Window* booklet put out by Great Western Railway transported him on a nostalgic journey from Paddington to Penzance. The descriptions unfolded the landscape so gently that he could almost imagine sitting in a first-class dining car with white tablecloths and flowers and lazily gazing out the window.

In 1924, Great Western Railway produced a travel guide describing points of interest that patrons could see out the window as the train made the 305-mile journey from London's Paddington Station to Penzance. Passengers could follow along as the English landscape unfolded before them.

The ground-level view and leisurely pace of the trains made for a chatty narrative, divided into six-mile increments, with landmarks numbered to correspond with the map on the facing page. Sometimes, the Great Western guide had to stretch for places to describe. In one section, it admitted, "Now London has some very pleasant western suburbs, but it is too much to expect to see them at their best from the train, for London has a habit—a very unwise one, considering the kind of first impression it gives to strangers arriving in the capital—of showing her worst side to the railway."

In another section, the pamphlet pointed out that the "most imposing feature of Hanwell is the great mental hospital of the County of London." Farther down the track, the key attraction was the "great Maypole margarine factory," and beyond that the Grand Junction Canal, "with bridges, barges and ducks all doing their best to make it picturesque." The descriptions were not meant to draw tourists to these places, but merely to offer things for passengers to muse on during the seven-hour journey.

PENTAGRAM PAPERS 15

THROUGH THE WINDOW

I first found *Through the Window* on my late father-in-law's bookshelf in Australia. Although seldom given to nostalgia, I found myself thinking of Paddington and the journey to Penzance.

What a pleasure it must have been to sit in a first class dining car with white tablecloth and flowers on the table looking out of a large picture window. This book would have enhanced the pleasure with its descriptions of the factories, churches, canals, hills and dales. The journey would have taken seven hours. For me the ironic comparison is the journey across the Atlantic, which I so often take, with a one in five chance of a window seat and then a miniature window with a view of the top of a wing. The intended relief from boredom is an 'in-flight' magazine full of ads for exercise machines and Sheraton Hotels.

It is interesting that the patron of the book was Great Western Railway. At that time, the British Railways were independent; London Midland Scottish, London North Eastern and Southern Railways. Each had its own personality and indeed the Great Western Railway was the most mystical and elite. It was to do with Brunel, who not only designed the railway, Paddington Station and the bridges but also homes for the railway workers. This book must have been another facet, however small, that helped develop that image.

In our opinion, *Through the Window* is a perfect example of good communication for two reasons. Firstly, it has an interesting idea, the sequential presentation of information planned to relate to an experience, and secondly, it is beautifully executed.

We have reprinted the first section, Paddington to Windsor.

Colin Forbes

Cover illustrations and drawings from the window are done by H. Powell. The engraving of Paddington Station is by E. Margaret Holman.

Compiled and produced for the Great Western Railway by Ed. J. Burrow & Co. Ltd. 1924; reprinted 1927.

Ed. J. Burrow & Co. Limited, Streatham Hill, London SW2 4TR [Tel: 01 674 1222 (PBX)]

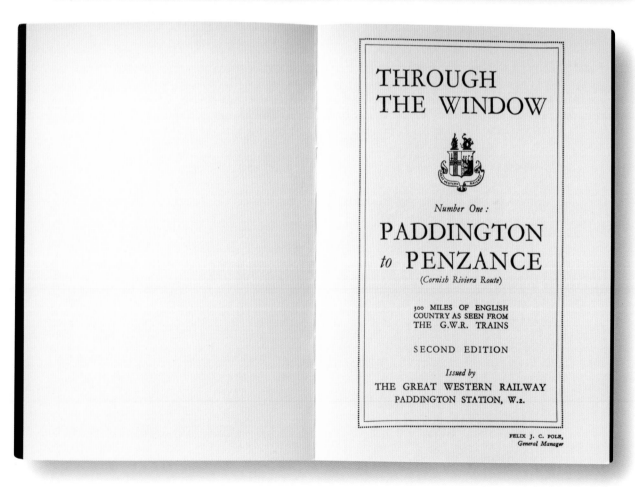

Colin Forbes found this 1924 travel guide worthy of reproduction as a Pentagram Paper because, for such a modest piece, it managed to parcel out information sequentially as the experience unfolded and execute it simply and beautifully.

"THE 10.30 LIMITED."

HOW TO USE "THROUGH THE WINDOW"

THE journey of 305 miles from Paddington to Penzance is much more than a means to an end. It is an experience thoroughly worth while for its own sake. It unfolds a vast stretch of English landscape in constantly changing panorama and traverses almost the entire breadth of England at its widest part.

In this book an attempt has been made to break up this long journey into its component parts in the geographical sense. Any such system of grouping is open to objections, but there seem to be good logical grounds for the following rough classification :

Within these main divisions, points and features of interest seen through the carriage windows are described in such detail as space will allow. Some tell their own story, others become interesting when one reads of origins and associations not obvious on the surface.

Each page of the detailed letterpress covers as nearly as possible six miles of the line and is faced by a map of the same section on which points of interest are identified by reference numbers corresponding to those used in the text. The terms left and right used throughout the book mean the left and right of a passenger who is sitting facing the engine.

The maps are to be read from the bottom upwards, as this makes their direction coincide with that of the train as the book is held by a passenger looking towards Penzance. The letterpress, however, is read in the ordinary way.

The fact that the famous " 10-30 Limited," the Cornish Riviera Express by which those who make the full journey from London to Penzance usually travel, makes a non-stop run from Paddington to Plymouth, a distance of 225 miles, is sufficient in itself to excite interest in the mechanical side of such a splendid achievement—in the powerful express locomotive and the finely-appointed corridor coaches behind it, in the splendid track which makes the journey pass so smoothly and with so little consciousness of terrific speed, in the pick-up water troughs and other pieces of equipment which represent the last word up to date in railway engineering.

In this book there is no room for any substantial measure of information about those things, but they are described in detail and admirably illustrated in another publication of the Great Western Railway, " The 10-30 Limited—a book for boys of all ages."

5

LONDON.

THE GATEWAY TO THE WEST

PADDINGTON STATION is London's great gateway to the West, and the fascination of travel begins from the moment one arrives beneath the vast curves of its great glass roof. The people on the platforms, the scraps of conversation, the destination boards on the trains, the labels on the luggage—all have a strong West Country flavour. A dash of naval uniform conjures up visions of distant Plymouth and Devonport. The characteristic patois of Devon and Somerset mingles with the dialect of West Cornwall, which has at times a quaint, musical note and brings into play local words that only a Cornishman would understand.

This long, swift journey from London to Land's End—or as near to it as makes no matter—has about it a certain savour of romance, a spice of adventure, which no amount of familiarity with railway travelling can destroy. Not only the great distance in itself—over 300 miles—but also the fact that so vast a stretch of it is taken at a single stride, helps to create the feeling that in stepping on to the footboard of the " 10-30 Limited " one is embarking upon an adventure, and that's a fine thing in itself.

No need to enquire which platform for the Cornish Riviera Express—Number One every time ! To experienced travellers, Paddington Station stands out among the London termini by a certain coherence of arrangement, and Platform Number One is in many ways a model of convenience, grouping together all the facilities one needs at the outset of a long journey.

One steps aboard the " Limited " with a sensation not far removed from that of boarding a sea-going ship. There is a certain irrevocability about it which makes the undertaking a vastly different one from a journey on the Underground, where you can change your mind and retrieve your position within a few minutes of starting. To put it in another way, this great journey to the West has something of the fascination of foreign travel. Land's End has a far-away sound when one is surrounded by the surging crowds and noisy bustle of London, but no farther away than London seems when one is walking the Promenade at Penzance.

And now steam is up, and a vast pile of luggage has been stowed away in the holds of the good ship " Limited," the last hand-shakes are taken and the last " Good-byes " said as the guard blows his whistle and waves his green flag, and dead on the stroke of 10-30 a.m. the long train begins to move and will not cease from moving until we draw into Plymouth North Road Station, 225 miles away, at 2.37 p.m. precisely. We shall, however, shake off several parts of our tail en route—" slip " coaches for Weymouth, Taunton, Ilfracombe, Minehead, Exeter and other intermediate places.

7

PADDINGTON TO EALING BROADWAY

THE first half-dozen miles of the journey from PADDINGTON (1) lie through the western suburbs of London. Now London has some very pleasant western suburbs, but it is too much to expect to see them at their best from the train, for London has a habit—a very unwise one, considering the kind of first impression it gives to strangers arriving in the capital—of showing her worst side to the railway. But Suburbia, with her tall houses blocking out wider views, forms only an infinitesimal stage of our more than 300 miles run to the West, and by the time one has got comfortably settled in one's seat the solid rampart of houses on either side of the line has been left behind.

ROYAL OAK STATION (2) and the important suburban station of WESTBOURNE PARK (3) are passed within the first two or three minutes and then some points of interest begin to appear on either side. On the right is a peep at KENSAL GREEN CEMETERY (4), where Thackeray, Leigh Hunt and other famous people are buried. Only one or two of the stones show from the railway, and the glimpse of trees rising above walls and fences is suggestive of a park rather than a cemetery.

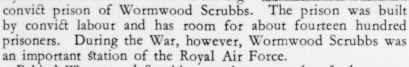

The large open space seen on the left, with a great airship shed upon it, is WORMWOOD SCRUBBS (5), and the large range of buildings behind in the barrack style of architecture are those of the big convict prison of Wormwood Scrubbs. The prison was built by convict labour and has room for about fourteen hundred prisoners. During the War, however, Wormwood Scrubbs was an important station of the Royal Air Force.

Behind Wormwood Scrubbs may be seen rather farther away some of the tall cupolas of the great Shepherd's Bush EXHIBITION BUILDINGS (6) which were used for the Franco-British, the Japan-British, and other exhibitions a few years before the War. The main line to Birmingham diverges to the right near here. At 4½ miles from Paddington we pass through the populous suburb of ACTON (7), which gives us a passing glimpse of open country looking across to the right towards the spire of HARROW-ON-THE-

HILL (8). But the view is soon shut off by the widespread brick-and-mortar of EALING (9), one of the largest and most important of the western suburbs.

EALING BROADWAY (10) is as far as the "Tube" trains venture out of London in this direction, and one or more of them is usually seen in the station to the right.

8

The narrative text is numbered to coincide with the map's points of interest. What's amusing by today's standards is that the map covers only a six-mile distance, and the first two landmarks appear just minutes after leaving the station.

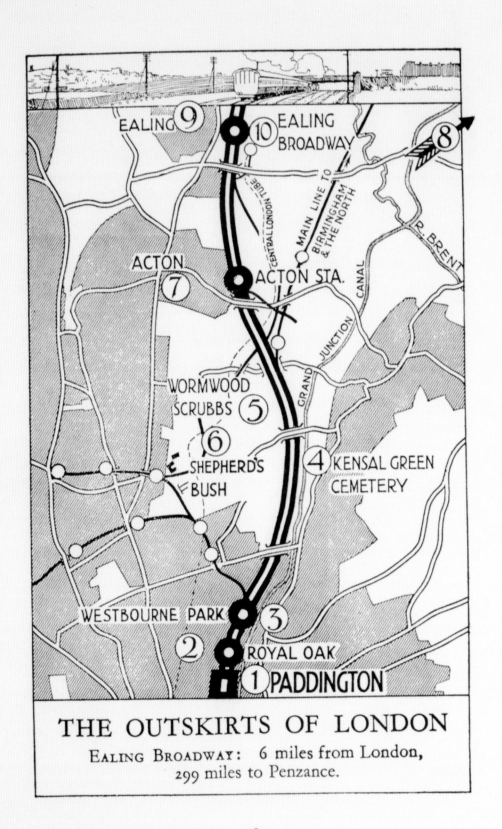

THE OUTSKIRTS OF LONDON

EALING BROADWAY: 6 miles from London,
299 miles to Penzance.

9

No. 8: **Views from Pentagram, New York**

Back Story

Shortly after partners Colin
Forbes and Peter Harrison
set up a Pentagram office
in New York, they leased
a space previously occupied
by an electrical fittings
wholesaler on the seven-
teenth floor of 212 Fifth
Avenue. When they first saw
it, all the windows were
boarded up so the whole-
saler could better display
his lighting fixtures. When
the panels were removed,
it came as a complete
surprise to face spectacular
views of the surrounding
buildings. What better way
to announce their move
into the new office than by
having Bruce Davidson,
one of the world's foremost
photographers, shoot out
every window?

When Pentagram moved onto the seventeenth floor of a building at Madison
Square Park in 1980, the staff became
privy to a view of Manhattan invisible to
passersby on the streets below. From
their lofty perch, the staff could see across the way to the
upper levels of other high-rises, which were crowned
with statues, abstract murals, and a delectable array of
towers, temples, and spires all around.

In the late nineteenth century when most of these
buildings were constructed, Madison Gardens where
Broadway crosses Fifth Avenue was considered a fashionable address, and its dramatic Flatiron Building
signaled the beginning of a new architecture. Each new
office tower was lovingly embellished with lyrical details
meant to be appreciated from an unobstructed distant
perspective. Seeing these elements as the architects had
intended them to be viewed motivated Colin Forbes
and Peter Harrison to propose a Pentagram Paper at the
next partners' meeting. They decided to ask Magnum
photographer Bruce Davidson, with whom Peter Harrison
was working at the time, to shoot the views from the
windows of Pentagram's new office.

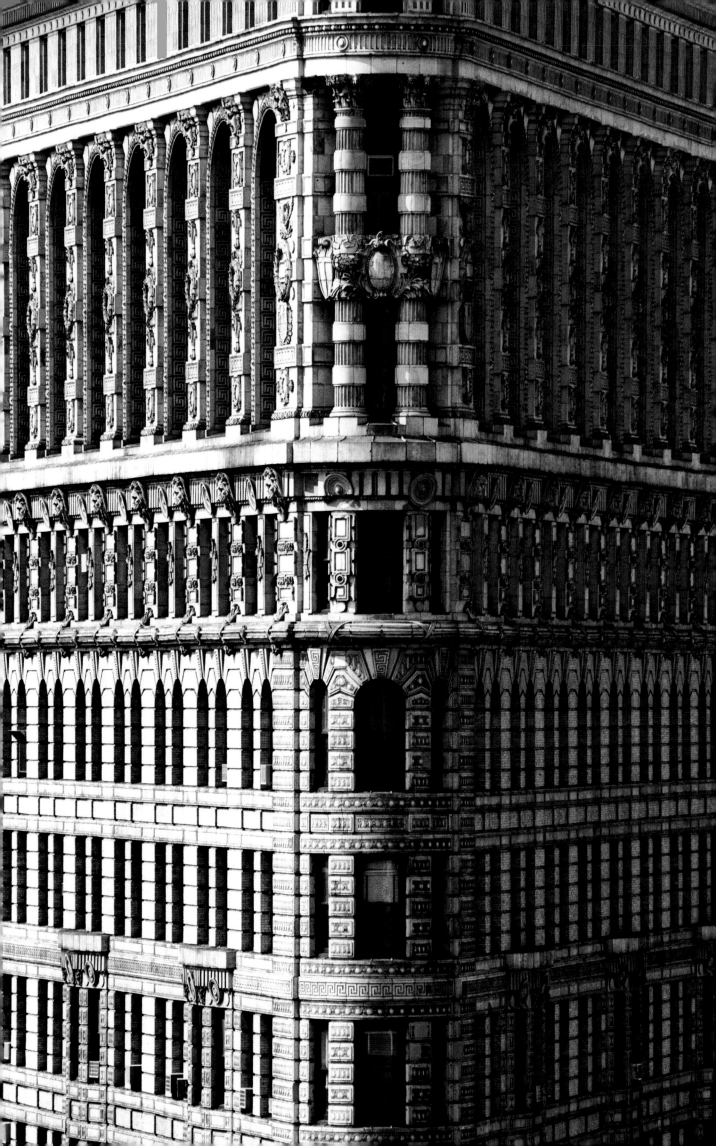

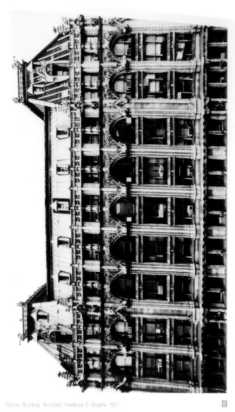

The most marvellous, romantic, energetic, squalid city in the world. New York is a crash course in architectural aesthetics. The city grows buildings, infinitely varied, cemented into an instant history. It grows, like a wild flower responding to every change of thought, of style and to the delicate ebb and flow of money. The flux of prosperity throws up vast edifices, and the ebbing of the life giving elixir leaves them, in a few years, shuttered and haunted ruins. Then romance begins to take over.

The great expansion, in the latter 19th century from the Battery northwards to Central Park filled the first forty streets with serious, orderly, apparently permanent buildings. They were in every possible style, but expressed only and accurately the power and energy of the 19th century. By 1900 the fashionable area was Madison Gardens, where Broadway crosses Fifth Avenue, and the Flatiron Building marked the beginning of the new architecture. All around were tall offices and lofts, and they hummed with a lively prosperity that faded in the 1920's.

The buildings remain, worn and grimy, but they now begin to take on the reassuring presence of a genuine history. They are suddenly valuable, because they have become irreplaceable. All that once irrelevant decoration, those totally useless statues perched up on the 19th floor, take on the glamour and the relevance of a Gothic Cathedral, a Baroque palace. Their role in the city, once an expression of everyday exuberance, now becomes a cheering exemplar.

Pentagram discovered this 17th floor loft overlooking the world's lint-filled navel, and moved in with great pleasure. Outside there are views and juxtapositions that continually invigorate: knights in armour, abstract murals and a delectable array of towers, temples and spires all round.

Bruce Davidson took the pictures from our windows. They are a very personal interpretation of the place; they show the variety of form and mood, the unexpected details but above all the sensation of miraculous height, floating among the pinnacles that adorn the city.

Theo Crosby

To give readers a sense of the awesome sights from every window, this Pentagram Paper was printed in a double-sided accordion fold, with the location of each building numbered to correspond with the isometric street drawing shown on the cover.

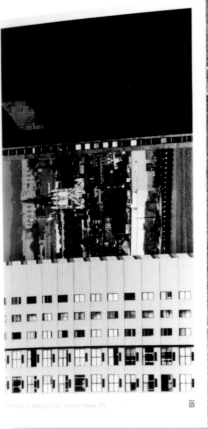

brun & Sons, 1891.   Consolidated Edison Company. Architect: Warren & Wetmore, 1929.   h Avenue th. Episcopal Church. Architect: F. Kerry, 1873.

icken, Lebrun & Sons, 1909.   105 Madison. Architect: Hellmuth Obata & Kassabaum, 1915.   225 5th Avenue. Architect: Francis H. Kimball & Harry E. Donnell, 1907.   St. James Building. Architect: Bruce Price, 1897-98.

No. 5: **The Palace of the League of Nations**

Architecture does not emerge from a barren landscape, but is informed by the events, technologies, and discoveries occurring at that time. Noting how these elements intersect intrigued architect and Pentagram partner Ron Herron, who delighted in considering entries in major architectural competitions in relation to other events. "It is extraordinary what diverse solutions come out of any architectural competition, ranging from academic historicism to open rejection of accepted aesthetic theory," Herron mused. "I have found it a rewarding exercise to put these solutions, in turn, into their historic and social contexts."

To illustrate his point for this Pentagram Paper, Herron chose the competition for the design of the Palace of the League of Nations, which took place in 1926–27 as the Heroic Period of modern architecture was coming to a close. The international competition attracted 377 entrants, including Le Corbusier, whose work was disqualified because it had not been drawn in ink.

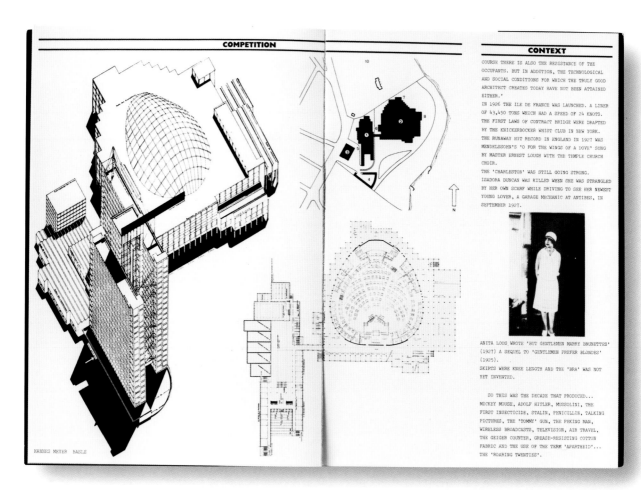

COURSE THERE IS ALSO THE RESISTANCE OF THE OCCUPANTS. BUT IN ADDITION, THE TECHNOLOGICAL AND SOCIAL CONDITIONS FOR WHICH THE TRULY GOOD ARCHITECT CREATES TODAY HAVE NOT BEEN ATTAINED EITHER.'

IN 1926 THE ILE DE FRANCE WAS LAUNCHED, A LINER OF 43,450 TONS WHICH HAD A SPEED OF 24 KNOTS. THE FIRST LAWS OF CONTRACT BRIDGE WERE DRAFTED BY THE KNICKERBOCKER WHIST CLUB IN NEW YORK. THE RUNAWAY HIT RECORD IN ENGLAND IN 1927 WAS MENDELSSOHN'S 'O FOR THE WINGS OF A DOVE' SUNG BY MASTER ERNEST LOUGH WITH THE TEMPLE CHURCH CHOIR.
THE 'CHARLESTON' WAS STILL GOING STRONG. ISADORA DUNCAN WAS KILLED WHEN SHE WAS STRANGLED BY HER OWN SCARF WHILE DRIVING TO SEE HER NEWEST YOUNG LOVER, A GARAGE MECHANIC AT ANTIBES, IN SEPTEMBER 1927.

ANITA LOOS WROTE 'BUT GENTLEMEN MARRY BRUNETTES' (1927) A SEQUEL TO 'GENTLEMEN PREFER BLONDES' (1925).
SKIRTS WERE KNEE LENGTH AND THE 'BRA' WAS NOT YET INVENTED.

SO THIS WAS THE DECADE THAT PRODUCED... MICKEY MOUSE, ADOLF HITLER, MUSSOLINI, THE FIRST INSECTICIDE, STALIN, PENICILLIN, TALKING PICTURES, THE 'TOMMY' GUN, THE PEKING MAN, WIRELESS BROADCASTS, TELEVISION, AIR TRAVEL, THE GEIGER COUNTER, GREASE-RESISTING COTTON FABRIC AND THE USE OF THE TERM 'APARTHEID'... THE 'ROARING TWENTIES'.

HANNES MEYER BASLE

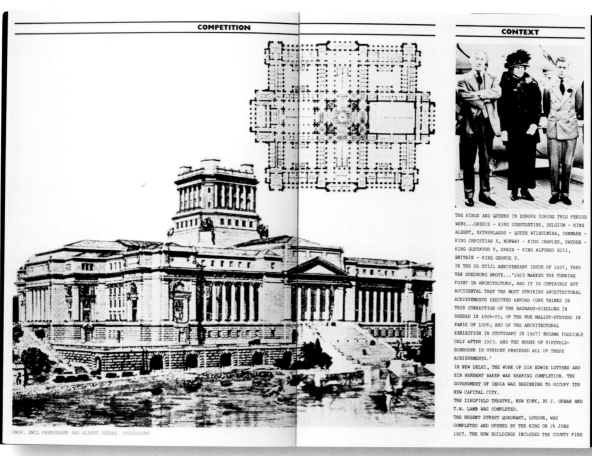

THE KINGS AND QUEENS IN EUROPE DURING THIS PERIOD WERE...GREECE - KING CONSTANTINE, BELGIUM - KING ALBERT, NETHERLANDS - QUEEN WILHELMINA, DENMARK - KING CHRISTIAN X, NORWAY - KING CHARLES, SWEDEN - KING GUSTAVUS V, SPAIN - KING ALFONSO XIII, BRITAIN - KING GEORGE V.
IN THE DE STIJL ANNIVERSARY ISSUE OF 1927, THEO VAN DOESBURG WROTE...'1923 MARKED THE TURNING POINT IN ARCHITECTURE, AND IT IS CERTAINLY NOT ACCIDENTAL THAT THE MOST STRIKING ARCHITECTURAL ACHIEVEMENTS EXECUTED ABROAD (ONE THINKS IN THIS CONNECTION OF THE BAUHAUS-SIEDLUNG IN DESSAU IN 1924-25; OF THE RUE MALLET-STEVENS IN PARIS OF 1926; AND OF THE ARCHITECTURAL EXHIBITION IN STUTTGART IN 1927) BECAME POSSIBLE ONLY AFTER 1923. AND THE HOUSE OF RIETVELD-SCHRODER IN UTRECHT PRECEDED ALL OF THESE ACHIEVEMENTS.'
IN NEW DELHI, THE WORK OF SIR EDWIN LUTYENS AND SIR HERBERT BAKER WAS NEARING COMPLETION. THE GOVERNMENT OF INDIA WAS BEGINNING TO OCCUPY ITS NEW CAPITAL CITY.
THE ZIEGFIELD THEATRE, NEW YORK, BY J. URBAN AND T.W. LAMB WAS COMPLETED.
THE REGENT STREET QUADRANT, LONDON, WAS COMPLETED AND OPENED BY THE KING ON 24 JUNE 1927. THE NEW BUILDINGS INCLUDED THE COUNTY FIRE

PROF. EMIL FAHRENKAMP AND ALBERT DENEKE DUSSELDORF

Each spread showed sketches entered into the Palace of the League of Nations architectural competition of 1926–27 and cited events occurring at the time. The winning entry (page 195) is now the United Nations building in Geneva.

LE CORBUSIER AND PIERRE JEANNERET COMPLETED THE
MAISON COOK. 1926.
THE FIRST LAUNCHING OF A LIQUID-FUELLED ROCKET
BY DR. ROBERT HITCHINGS GODDARD TOOK PLACE ON
16 MARCH 1926 AT AUBURN, MASSACHUSETTS. IT
REACHED AN ALTITUDE OF 12.5 METRES AND TRAVELLED
A DISTANCE OF 56 METRES.

THE BAUHAUS AT DESSAU, DESIGNED BY WALTER GROPIUS,
WAS COMPLETED IN DECEMBER 1926, AND FORMALLY
INAUGURATED ON DECEMBER 4. THE INAUGURATION
CELEBRATIONS INCLUDED AN EXHIBITION, LECTURES
AND MOTION PICTURES, AS WELL AS A DANCE IN THE
NEW BUILDING. FIVE FORMER STUDENTS, JOSEF ALBERS,
HERBERT BAYER, MARCEL BREUER, HINNERK SCHEPER AND
JOOST SCHMIDT WERE APPOINTED MASTERS.

BING CROSBY MADE HIS FIRST COMMERCIAL RECORDING
ON 18 OCTOBER 1926. THIS WAS 'I'VE GOT THE GIRL'
MASTER NO. W142785 (TAKE 5) ISSUED ON THE
COLUMBIA LABEL.
THE SONG 'STARDUST' WAS WRITTEN BY HOAGY
CARMICHAEL, IN 1927, AND HAS SINCE BEEN RECORDED
SOME 900-1000 TIMES IN THE U.S. ALONE.
THE WORLD HEAVYWEIGHT BOXING CHAMPION WAS GENE
TURNNEY.
THE MERSEY TUNNEL IN LIVERPOOL WAS UNDER
CONSTRUCTION.
THE MODEL 'T' FORD (1908-27) REACHED A PRODUCTION
RECORD OF 15,007,034 CARS.

MESSRS. J.E.P. HENDRICKX AND J.M.E. DE LIGNE BRUSSELS

HAKON AHLBERG STOCKHOLM

JAMES BURFORD A.R.I.B.A. GREAT BRITAIN

IN 1927 THE INTERNATIONAL COMPETITION FOR THE
DESIGN OF THE PALACE OF THE LEAGUE OF NATIONS,
GENEVA, TOOK PLACE, WITH ENTRIES BY SCHINDLER
AND NEUTRA, HANNES MEYER, LE CORBUSIER ETC......
LE CORBUSIER'S ENTRY WAS DISQUALIFIED BECAUSE IT
HAD NOT BEEN DRAWN IN INK!
AND...

THE GENERAL STRIKE BEGAN IN GREAT BRITAIN. MAY
1926.
THE FIRST OF SEVERAL ATTEMPTS TO ASSASSINATE
BENITO MUSSOLINI TOOK PLACE. APRIL 1926.
THE COUNCIL FOR THE PRESERVATION OF RURAL
ENGLAND WAS ESTABLISHED.
CONSTANT LAMBERT WROTE MUSIC FOR DIAGHILEV'S
BALLET 'ROMEO AND JULIET'- THE FIRST ENGLISH
COMPOSER TO BE COMMISSIONED.

J.L. BAIRD DEMONSTRATED TELEVISION IN SOHO,
LONDON. JANUARY 1926.
JACK HOBBS SCORED SIXTEEN CENTURIES IN FIRST
CLASS CRICKET. SUMMER 1926.
QUEEN ELIZABETH II WAS BORN. APRIL 1926.
T.E. LAWRENCE'S 'SEVEN PILLARS OF WISDOM' WAS
PUBLISHED - AS A SUBSCRIBER'S EDITION. ABOUT
ONE HUNDRED SUBSCRIPTION COPIES WERE PUBLISHED
AT THIRTY GUINEAS EACH AND WITHIN A FEW WEEKS
SUBSCRIBERS WHO WERE WILLING TO SELL THEIR
COPIES COULD GET BETWEEN £300 AND £400 FOR THEM.

CARLO BROGGI (ENGINEER) WITH MESSRS. GIUSEPPE VACCARO AND LUIGI FRANZI ROME

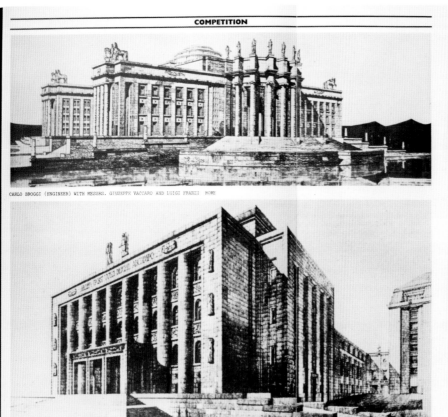

M. PIACENTINI, G. RAPISARDI AND A. MAZZONI ROME

No. 33: **The Slide Rule Vanishes**

Back Story

While working with Lance Knobel, a writer and strategy advisor, on a project for the World Economic Forum, partner John McConnell discovered that Knobel collected slide rules, once a ubiquitous tool found in nearly every home. Sadly, fewer and fewer people had ever held a slide rule in their hands, much less knew how to work one. Even though its functional usefulness was outdated, the slide rule, in all its many variations, was an object of beauty—a reason to celebrate its history and contribution to mankind.

Before there were computer geeks, there were slide-rule geeks. For nearly 350 years, the slide rule was considered the ultimate in calculating power—that is, until Hewlett-Packard launched the first hand-held calculator, the HP35, in 1972.

Slide rules work because of logarithms, which were invented by John Napier, a Scottish mathematician and theologian, early in the seventeenth century. Searching for a way to do multiplication and division problems using addition and subtraction, Napier arrived at a method of substituting artificial numbers (logarithms, or logs) for real numbers. Circa 1625, English astronomer Edmund Gunter found a way to visualize Napier's logarithms by spacing numbers at intervals proportionate to their log values. This approach was carried a step further by the noted mathematician Reverend William Oughtred, who had the idea of combining two Gunter scales and doing calculations simply by sliding them back and forth.

Over the centuries, the use of the slide rule became required study in high school advanced-math courses, essential preparation for becoming a scientist or engineer. No sooner had the hand-held calculator appeared, however, than the slide rule all but disappeared.

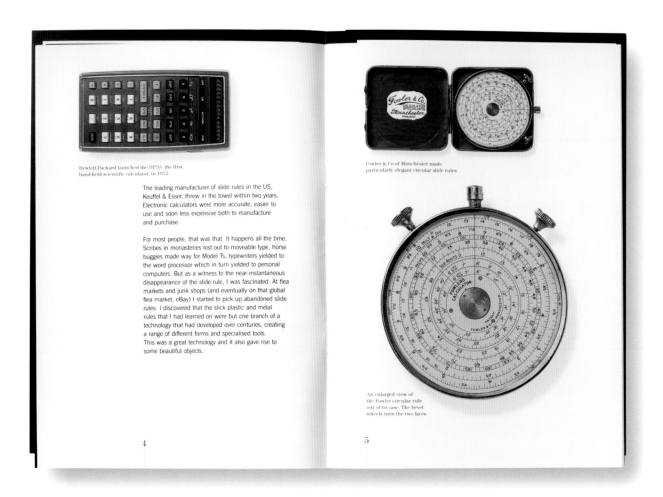

Hewlett-Packard launched the HP35, the first
hand-held scientific calculator, in 1972

Fowler & Co of Manchester made
particularly elegant circular slide rules

An enlarged view of
the Fowler circular rule
out of its case. The bevel
wheels turn the two faces

The leading manufacturer of slide rules in the US,
Keuffel & Esser, threw in the towel within two years.
Electronic calculators were more accurate, easier to
use and soon less expensive both to manufacture
and purchase.

For most people, that was that. It happens all the time.
Scribes in monasteries lost out to moveable type, horse
buggies made way for Model Ts, typewriters yielded to
the word processor which in turn yielded to personal
computers. But as a witness to the near-instantaneous
disappearance of the slide rule, I was fascinated. At flea
markets and junk shops (and eventually on that global
flea market, eBay) I started to pick up abandoned slide
rules. I discovered that the slick plastic and metal
rules that I had learned on were but one branch of a
technology that had developed over centuries, creating
a range of different forms and specialised tools.
This was a great technology and it also gave rise to
some beautiful objects.

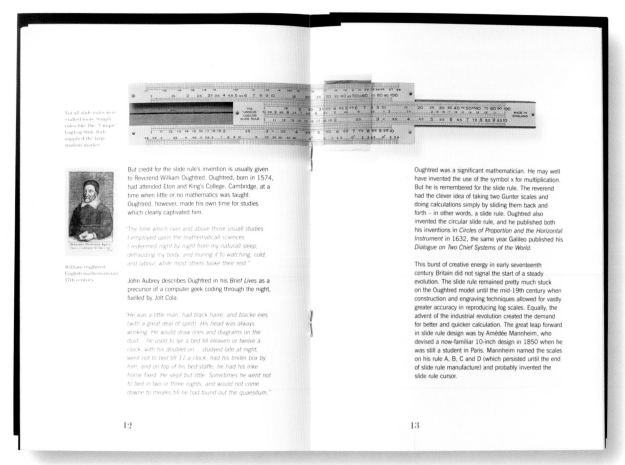

Not all slide rules were
exalted tools. Simple
rules like The 'Unique'
Log-Log Slide Rule
supplied the large
student market

William Oughtred
English mathematician
17th century

But credit for the slide rule's invention is usually given
to Reverend William Oughtred. Oughtred, born in 1574,
had attended Eton and King's College, Cambridge, at a
time when little or no mathematics was taught.
Oughtred, however, made his own time for studies
which clearly captivated him.

"The time which over and above those usuall studies
I employed upon the mathematicall sciences
I redeemed night by night from my naturall sleep,
defrauding my body, and inuring it to watching, cold,
and labour, while most others tooke their rest."

John Aubrey describes Oughtred in his *Brief Lives* as a
precursor of a computer geek coding through the night,
fuelled by Jolt Cola:

"He was a little man, had black haire, and blacke eies
(with a great deal of spirit). His head was always
working. He would draw lines and diagrams on the
dust ... he used to lye a bed till eleaven or twelve a
clock, with his doublet on ... studyed late at night,
went not to bed till 11 a clock, had his tinder box by
him, and on top of his bed-staffe, he had his inke
horne fixed. He slept but little. Sometimes he went not
to bed in two or three nights, and would not come
downe to meales till he had found out the quaesitum."

Oughtred was a significant mathematician. He may well
have invented the use of the symbol x for multiplication.
But he is remembered for the slide rule. The reverend
had the clever idea of taking two Gunter scales and
doing calculations simply by sliding them back and
forth – in other words, a slide rule. Oughtred also
invented the circular slide rule, and he published both
his inventions in *Circles of Proportion and the Horizontal
Instrument* in 1632, the same year Galileo published his
Dialogue on Two Chief Systems of the World.

This burst of creative energy in early seventeenth
century Britain did not signal the start of a steady
evolution. The slide rule remained pretty much stuck
on the Oughtred model until the mid-19th century when
construction and engraving techniques allowed for vastly
greater accuracy in reproducing log scales. Equally, the
advent of the industrial revolution created the demand
for better and quicker calculation. The great leap forward
in slide rule design was by Amédée Mannheim, who
devised a now-familiar 10-inch design in 1850 when he
was still a student in Paris. Mannheim named the scales
on his rule A, B, C and D (which persisted until the end
of slide rule manufacture) and probably invented the
slide rule cursor.

The slide rule had straight, circular, and cylindrical variations. Some types were more suited to certain tasks than others. The
electronic slide rule enables calculations of voltage and resistance; others helped gunners figure the right angle of inclination.

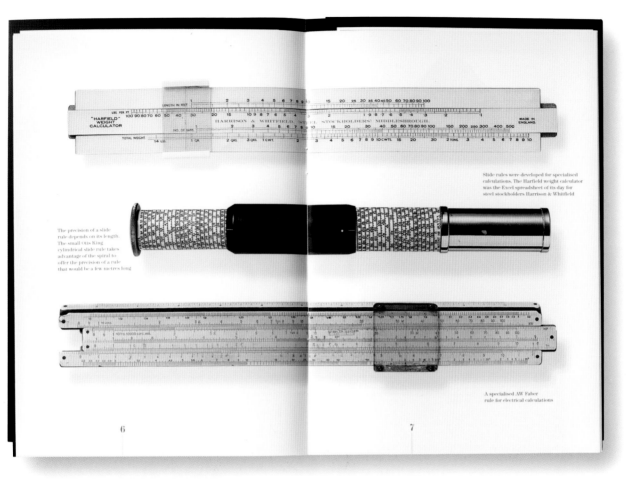

Slide rules were developed for specialised calculations. The Harfield weight calculator was the Excel spreadsheet of its day for steel stockholders Harrison & Whitfield

The precision of a slide rule depends on its length. The small Otis King cylindrical slide rule takes advantage of the spiral to offer the precision of a rule that would be a few metres long

A specialised AW Faber rule for electrical calculations

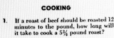

COOKING

1. If a roast of beef should be roasted 12 minutes to the pound, how long will it take to cook a 5¾ pound roast?

   Answer: $12 \times 5.75 = 69$ minutes

   $= \dfrac{69}{60} = 1$ hour, 9 minutes.

TELEPHONE

1. A movie fan in New York City calls her favorite star in Hollywood. If the rate in the day time is $6.25 for 3 minutes with $2.15 a minute for each additional minute, plus 20¢ Federal tax, and the call lasts 6 minutes, what is the total charge?

   Answer:

   $(6.25 + .20 + [2.15 \times 3]) = \$12.90$

   Set the left-hand index of the *C* scale over 3 on the *D* scale. Move the runner to 2.15 on the *C* scale and read the answer $6.45 on the *D* scale under the hair-line. Add the other two terms for the final result.

every part as light and as highly stressed as possible… there is little room for error – in the computer's calculations, in the parts manufacturers' products, or in the construction workers' execution of the design. Thus computer-optimized structures may be marginally or least-safe designs."

Magnitude is an equally serious loss. The need to work out magnitude before producing an answer requires an understanding of how a calculation works. It is not sufficient to do the prescribed steps; there has to be an understanding of what you were doing. Today, it is a common experience to be presented with something plainly wrong, only to be told, "Oh, that's what the computer says."

Of course, it is perfectly possible to get wrong answers from a slide rule. But by its very nature, the user is required to understand how to work through a problem. Edward Tenner, in his book *Why Things Bite Back: Technology and the Revenge of Unintended Consequences*, explains the shift.

"We cease to be tool users and, in [museum curator James] Blackaby's phrase, begin to be tool managers. We direct and control processes that take place rather than shape them. Blackaby has contrasted the

leather-cased ivory slide rule presented to him as a college freshman by his father with the electronic calculator he has since come to use. One requires human judgment, experience, and the constant exercise of skill; the other simply executes the operations it is programmed to do."

Those of us who love slide rules are by definition not Luddites. It's the tactile nature of the technology that excites, rather than a revulsion against the technologies that replaced it. There were gains provided by electronic calculators. Our work, lives and society are being dramatically transformed – and I believe generally improved – through near-ubiquitous computing. But there are losses from the slide rule age that are more than nostalgia. It's better to be a tool user than a tool manager.

Halden Calculex pocket
calculator, in its convenient
leather case with manual

As beautiful and complex as a fine pocket watch, slide rules are works of art and marvels of science.

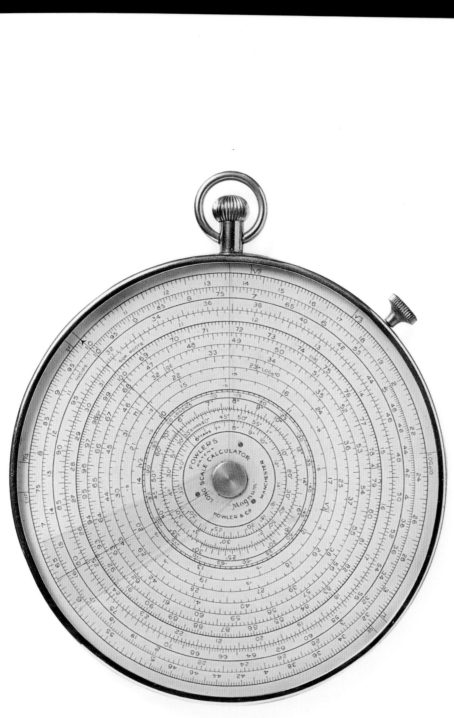

Fowler's Magnum long scale
calculator, shown life size.
The traditional letters for scales
are replaced by helpful definitions:
sqr roots, sines, tans etc

9

No. 11: **The City of Tomorrow: Model 1937**

Back Story

This Pentagram Paper came about through partner Colin Forbes' acquaintance with Jeffrey L. Meikle, a professor of American Studies at the University of Texas at Austin. Meikle had just written *Twentieth Century Limited: Industrial Design in America, 1925– 1939*. In the process of researching the book, he had acquired a number of unpublished photographs and papers documenting Norman Bel Geddes' creation of the City of Tomorrow. The material, Meikle told Forbes, was not substantial enough to turn into a book but was fascinating nonetheless. Forbes agreed, and Meikle wrote the essay for the Pentagram Paper.

Norman Bel Geddes was leading the effort to establish industrial design as a profession in 1937 when he was hired by the J. Walter Thompson advertising agency to create a model of the "City of Tomorrow" for a Shell Oil advertising campaign. Bel Geddes was already keenly interested in urban planning.

Asked to depict how traffic would flow in the year 1960, Bel Geddes embraced the assignment with zeal, trying to pinpoint and understand problems that cities of the future would face. For the advertising series, he conceived of an interstate highway system and designed a metropolis, which he rendered in a scale model that represented approximately the width of Manhattan. In his utopian world, multilane interstate highways bypassed cities, which were linked by feeder highways. In the urban area itself, high-speed expressway intersections and pedestrian bridges kept traffic flowing, while keeping cars and people on foot safely apart.

In 1937, Shell Oil presented Bel Geddes' model city in advertisements that carried the headline: "This is the City of Tomorrow. Pedestrians, Express Traffic, Local Traffic—each will be given a clear path by 1960— predicts Norman Bel Geddes, authority on future trends." Interestingly, the city that Bel Geddes imagined approximates what we see today, but it is far from utopian.

each will be given a clear path by 1960 – predicts Norman Bel Geddes, authority on future trends." Accompanying Garrison's startling photograph were brief discussions of the model's three main traffic elements. Readers were urged to remember that even if "traffic delays and confusion seem hopeless…men of vision are working on the problem" by "planning city streets and country highways free from stop and go." In the meantime, however, motorists could "meet today's driving problem TODAY" by using Super-Shell gasoline, which had been chemically engineered to be "motor-digestible" and completely convertible into power even at the frustrating speeds of stop and go driving.

Subsequent advertisements took up only a single page, but the main themes remained the same, subject to minor variations. "In the City of Tomorrow," according to one version, "you'll swing into Main Street at 50", and if that image seemed a bit too reckless, especially to worried parents, the next ad in the series soothed any ruffled feathers by promising "No Stops because of Children playing in the Streets – In the City of Tomorrow." Typography and layout of many of the Life advertisements imitated that of the magazine's regular features. This device lent added authority to Bel Geddes's visualization of the future, especially in one instance when an ad followed directly after an article on the film Dead End – in which Bel Geddes figured prominently as designer of the original play's stage set. One curious change in the advertisements did occur as the campaign progressed to its conclusion. Photographs

forms of popular architecture document the Depression decade's obsession with expressive, almost baroque images of technology. And our own obsession appears most poignantly in the flattery of imitation. Many American cities now boast multi-form towers of reflective glass which could have been taken from the imaginative renderings of Hugh Ferriss. Shopping malls, with their low, curving blockhouse exteriors and their flowing, often metallic interiors, seem inspired by the world's fairs of fifty years ago. At the drop of a credit card, we can surround ourselves with furnishings and accessories designed in a "high-tech" manner which suggests that we too, like the upper class of the Depression years, can live in a future world made manifest today.

Ironically, however, these borrowings and references do not imply true belief in utopian possibilities. Rather they reveal profound nostalgia for a time past when one could indeed look boldly forward – even from the depth of economic chaos. We can no longer honestly and simply do so. We can, however, appreciate the panache with which the designers of the 1930's set out to plan and reshape everything, on whatever scale, from the smallest, most inconsequential object to the largest, most complex metropolis. And no one exhibited greater panache than industrial designer Norman Bel Geddes, who in 1936 began envisioning "the City of Tomorrow," circa 1960. Our nostalgia for his vision is all the more poignant because by 1960 we had indeed arrived in an approximation of his city, while coming no closer to utopia.

Before Norman Bel Geddes was hired by General Motors to create the Futurama exhibit for the 1938 New York World's Fair, he conceived of the City of Tomorrow for a 1937 Shell Oil advertising campaign, shown photographed in a studio (top left).

13

order to relieve the strain of night driving. These vast highways would bypass cities and towns, which would be linked into the system by feeder highways, some as many as twelve lanes across. Although Bel Geddes worked out this transcontinental system in intricate detail and provided the Thompson agency with renderings, maps, and, in some instances, actual plans for construction, he and his staff concentrated most of their effort on solving the urban traffic problem. After all, the typical motorist in New York City could expect to travel no faster than his grandfather had done with a horse and buggy.

It was William Day who on November 12, in conference, offered the solution which continued to intrigue Bel Geddes for several weeks. "The simplest method of eliminating cars in New York City or elsewhere," he suggested, "would be to pass a law prohibiting private ownership." While such a measure would obviously have worked, he concluded that it "would not make a good ad…because it tends too much toward the socialistic." Not only did Americans value their newly attained mobility too dearly, but the executives of Shell Oil could hardly have been expected to approve an idea which would cut into their gasoline sales. Bel Geddes, on the other hand, admired simplicity if it could be had on a grand enough scale. Refining Day's hastily withdrawn idea a bit, he suggested placing a "huge city-owned parking terminal on the edge of the city," from which office workers and shoppers would commute in vans carrying from twelve to fifteen passengers.

Manhattan of about 1960, with a high-speed expressway intersection and pedestrian bridges at local street intersections created on Day.

17

products would streamline the flow of goods from producers to consumers by overcoming sales resistance. McClintock's four traffic "frictions" included "medial" (two-way traffic without separation); "marginal" (pedestrians, parked cars, mail boxes, and so on); "intersectional"; and "internal-stream" (vehicles going in the same direction at different speeds). To eliminate the vast majority of traffic accidents and causes of delay, simply overcome the four frictions, according to the theory. And to do that, one utilized "the principles of traffic hydraulics by delivering traffic as in a sealed conduit past all conflicting eddies and crosscurrents." [3] On the surface at least, Bel Geddes and McClintock were kindred spirits, members of a generation which conceived of efficiency as a matter of eliminating friction and streamlining the flow in whatever field of endeavor.

When McClintock visited the designer's office, they found that they were essentially in agreement over the shape of the interstate system needed by the United States, though the highway planner disliked the idea of 100-mile-an-hour lanes. They did not agree, however, on the best way in which to end urban congestion. Speaking with perhaps more common sense than Bel Geddes sometimes mustered, McClintock observed that fringe parking would never work because people would never put up with having to transfer from one mode of travel to another in mid-journey. Furthermore, New York City contained a large "submerged market" for the automobile industry – people who did not then own cars but who would purchase them as soon as their use became more

High office towers, dominating the tiny people and vehicles below, seemed to be the true inhabitants of the city.

Bel Geddes built a six-foot triangular model of Manhattan with thousands of basic building types, eleven thousand vehicles, and ninety thousand metal pins representing pedestrians. The model, exhibited across the country, has since disappeared.

No. 35: **Tin Tabernacles and Other Buildings**

Back Story

At a birthday party for a mutual friend, partner David Hillman ran into British photographer and filmmaker Alasdair Ogilvie and gave him a copy of the latest Pentagram Paper. Ogilvie took one look at it and told Hillman, "I have just the topic for you." As it turned out, Ogilvie had spent the last twenty years recording the dying traces of a once-popular, but nearly forgotten, building technique—corrugated tin tabernacles. Several of the buildings shot by Ogilvie have collapsed or been demolished since the photographs were taken. His photographs captured their austere beauty and transported one back to an earlier, more innocent time.

Scattered across Britain and the British Empire are a number of humble churches, clad in corrugated iron, that date back to the late nineteenth and early twentieth centuries. Sold in kit form through catalogs, these so-called "tin tabernacles" were meant to provide inexpensive temporary shelter and made no pretense of being great architecture.

Invented in 1844 by Phoenix Iron Works in England, the corrugated sheet metal was manufactured by flattening iron bars between giant rollers. It quickly found a market when the California gold rush of 1849 and the Australian gold find of 1851 spurred demand for building materials. Strong, lightweight, and portable, prefabricated sheet-metal buildings—from grain silos to houses—were easy to mass produce and ship to any part of the world. In 1854 alone, some thirty thousand buildings were shipped to Australia. Stepped-up production in coal and iron ore refineries in isolated and rural areas of Britain also triggered a population explosion that created an urgent need for churches and schools in new communities. Most of the corrugated-iron buildings have rusted away, with the exception of some tin tabernacles that have been fondly preserved by their congregations.

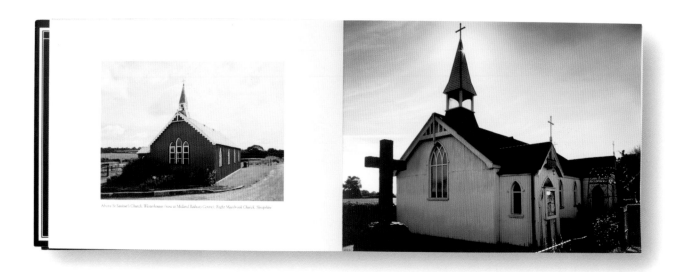

Above: St Saviour's Church, Westerhouse (now at Midland Railway Centre); Right: Marebrook Church, Shropshire

Above: Shepherd's Caravan, Aston Tirrold, Oxfordshire; Right: Shepherd's Caravan, Bibury, Gloucestershire

Corrugated galvanized iron churches, ordered through catalogs, were meant to be temporary. A prefab iron church could cost from £150 for a 150-seat chapel to £500 for a 350-seat chapel—a bargain compared to conventional building materials.

Above: All Saints, Dilton Marsh, Wiltshire. Right: Alkington Church, Somerset

Above: Stable, Ullenwood, Gloucestershire. Right: Barn, Leicestershire

Above: Railway shed, Raglan, Gwent. Left: Garage, Wheatly, Oxfordshire

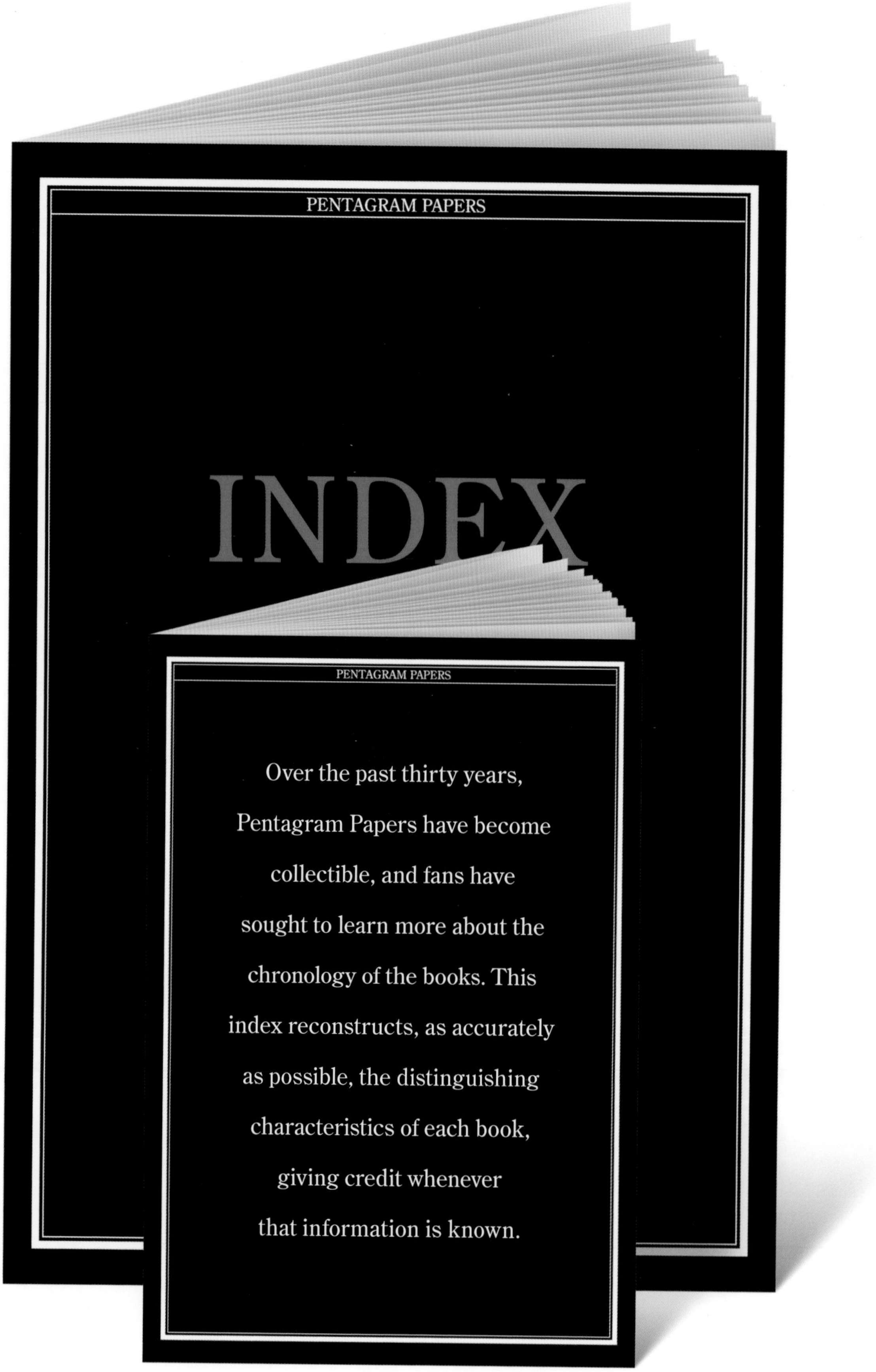

INDEX

PENTAGRAM PAPERS

Over the past thirty years,

Pentagram Papers have become

collectible, and fans have

sought to learn more about the

chronology of the books. This

index reconstructs, as accurately

as possible, the distinguishing

characteristics of each book,

giving credit whenever

that information is known.

**No. 1: ABC: A Dictionary
of Graphic Clichés**
Year: *1975, London*
Partner: *John McConnell*
Design/Photos/Text:
*Philip Thompson and
Peter Davenport*

**No. 2:
The Pessimist Utopia**
Year: *1975, London*
Partner: *Theo Crosby*
Design: *John McConnell*
Photos: *Jessica Strang*
Text: *Theo Crosby*

**No. 3: Brushes
and Brooms**
Year: *1976, London*
Partner: *John McConnell*
Design/Text: *Lou P. Klein*

No. 4: Face to Face
Year: *1977, London*
Partner: *John McConnell*
Design/Photos:
Jean Edouard Robert
Text: *Irwin Dermer*

**No. 5: The Palace of
the League of Nations**
Year: *1978, London*
Partner: *Ron Herron*
Design: *John McConnell*
Text: *Ron Herron*

**No. 6: Would You Care to
Make a Contribution?**
Year: *1979, London*
Partner/Design:
John McConnell
Text: *Brian Love*
Note: *Last page is full-color
accordion fold*

**No. 7: Ragazzini:
Photographs of Bomarzo**
Year: *1980, London*
Partner/Design:
John McConnell
Photos: *Enzo Ragazzini*
Text: *Theo Crosby*
Note: *Individual photos
wrapped in glassine*

**No. 8: Views From
Pentagram, New York**
Year: *1981, New York*
Partner: *Colin Forbes*
Design: *Peter Harrison*
Photos: *Bruce Davidson*
Text: *Theo Crosby*
Map: *Pictorial Maps, Inc.*
Note: *Accordion fold format*

**No. 9: Unilever House:
Towards a New Ornament**
Year: *1983, London*
Partner: *Theo Crosby*
Design: *John McConnell*
Photos: *Ken Kirkwood
and John Stone*
Text: *Theo Crosby*

**No. 10:
1211 North LaSalle**
Year: *1983, New York*
Partner: *Colin Forbes*
Design: *John McConnell*
Photos/Text:
François Robert

**No. 11: The City of
Tomorrow: Model 1937**
Year: *1984, London*
Partner/Design:
John McConnell
Photos: *Richard Garrison*
Text: *Jeffrey L. Meikle*

**No. 12: Olivier Mourgue's
Little Theatre of Design**
Year: *1985, London*
Partner/Design:
John McConnell
Photos: *Jon Naar*
Text: *Olivier Mourgue*
Translation:
Mark Thompson

No. 13:
Imprimeries Clandestines
Year: *1986, London*
Partner/Design:
John McConnell
Photos: *Robert Doisneau*
Text: *Reprint from* Le Point
Translation: *Mark Thompson*

No. 14: Stars & Stripes
Year: *1987, San Francisco*
Partner/Design:
Kit Hinrichs
Photos: *Barry Robinson*
Text: *Delphine Hirasuna*
Note: *500 copies with
an actual toothpick flag
affixed to cover*

**No. 15: Through
the Window**
Year: *1988, New York*
Partner/Design:
Colin Forbes
Illustrations: *H. Powell*
Intro: *Colin Forbes*
Text: *Reprint of* Through
the Window *by Ed. J. Burrow*

No. 16:
Kingswalden Notes
Year: *1989, London*
Partner/Design:
John McConnell
Illustrations/Text:
Quinlan Terry
Note: *Horizontal format*

No. 17:
The Many Faces of Mao
Year: *1989, San Francisco*
Partner: *Linda Hinrichs*
Design: *Linda Hinrichs
and Natalie Kitamura*
Photos: *Barry Robinson*
Text: *Delphine Hirasuna*

No. 18: Skeleton Closet
Year: *1990, New York*
Partner: *Woody Pirtle*
Design: *Woody Pirtle
and Matt Heck*
Photos: *William Whitehurst*
Intro: *Woody Pirtle
and Sarah Haun*

**No. 19: Purple,
White and Green**
Year: *1992, London*
Partner/Design:
John McConnell
Text: *Diane Atkinson*
Note: *Accordion fold format*

No. 20: Architecture
Year: *1993, New York*
Partner/Design:
Michael Bierut
Intro: *Michael Bierut*
Text: *Reprint of* Architec-
ture *by Lewis Mumford*

No. 21: Crop Circles
Year: *1993, London*
Partner: *John McConnell*
Design: *Julia Alldridge*
Photos: *George Wingfield
and Michael Glickman*
Diagrams/Text:
Michael Glickman

No. 22: Architectural Toys
Year: *1995, New York*
Partner: *James Biber*
Design: *Paula Scher*
Photos: *John Paul Endress*
Text: *James Biber*
Note: *Embossed cover*

No. 23: Cigar Papers
Year: *1995, London*
Partner/Design:
John McConnell
Photos: *Amanda Clement
and Nick Turner*
Text: *Juliet Barclay*
Note: *Foil stamp cover*

No. 24: The Arms of Paris
Year: *1996, London*
Partner/Design:
David Hillman
Photos/Text:
Claude Bestel
Note: *Embossed cover*

No. 25: Souvenir Albums
Year: *1996, San Francisco*
Partner/Design:
Kit Hinrichs
Photos: *Bob Esparza*
Text: *Delphine Hirasuna*
Note: *Includes miniature accordion fold album*

No. 26: On Pride and Prejudice in the Arts
Year: *1997, London*
Partner: *John McConnell*
Design: *Ron Costley*
Text: *Sir Ernst Gombrich*

No. 27: Nifty Places: The Australian Rural Mailbox
Year: *1998, London*
Partner: *David Hillman*
Design: *David Hillman and Lisa Enebeis*
Photos/Text: *Cal Swann*
Note: *Photo on both front and back cover*

No. 28: Of Money and the Divine
Year: *2000, New York*
Partner/Design:
Michael Bierut
Photos: *Various*
Text: *Tad Crawford*
Note: *Foil stamp cover*

No. 29: Savoy Lights
Year: *2000, London*
Partner: *John Rushworth*
Design: *John Rushworth and John Dowling*
Photos: *Phil Sayer*
Text: *Graham Vickers*

No. 30: Doo-Wop Commercial Architecture
Year: *2001, New York*
Partner/Design:
Michael Bierut
Photos: *Dorothy Kresz*
Text: *Jonathan van Meter*

No. 31: Hinagata: Kimono Pattern Books
Year: *2002, San Francisco*
Partner: *Kit Hinrichs*
Design: *Kit Hinrichs and Takayo Muroga*
Photos: *Terry Heffernan*
Text: *Delphine Hirasuna*
Note: *French fold binding*

No. 32: No Waste
Year: *2003, London*
Partner/Design:
Fernando Gutiérrez
Photos: *Ernesto Oroza*
Text: *Alex Marashian*
Note: *French fold binding; die-cut cover*

No. 33: The Slide Rule Vanishes
Year: *2004, London*
Partner: *John McConnell*
Design: *John McConnell and Zach John*
Photos: *Nick Turner*
Text: *Lance Knobel*

No. 34: Monografías
Year: *2005, New York*
Partner/Design:
Michael Bierut
Text: *Armin Vit*

No. 35: Tin Tabernacles and Other Buildings
Year: *2006, London*
Partner/Design:
David Hillman
Photos/Text:
Alasdair Olgilvie
Note: *Horizontal format*

No. 36: Marks of Africa
Year: *2006, London*
Partner: *John McConnell*
Design: *John McConnell and Zach John*
Renderings:
Fernando Medina
Text: *David Gibbs*

Special Thanks

Pentagram Papers could not have existed without the unique contributions of hundreds of designers, photographers, illustrators, architects, writers, historians, researchers, collectors, and craftspeople. Special thanks to writer Delphine Hirasuna, designer Myrna Newcomb, photographer Barry Robinson, and project manager Yael Wulfhart, together with Michael Carabetta, Alan Rapp, and the staff of Chronicle for their collaboration on this book. Thanks also to Inga Talmantienė and Karen Montgomery.

Designed by Kit Hinrichs
Photography by Barry Robinson, unless otherwise noted

Typeset in Century Old Style, Franklin Gothic, and News Gothic.

First published in the United Kingdom in 2006 by
Thames & Hudson Ltd, 181A High Holborn,
London WC1V 7QX

www.thamesandhudson.com

British Library Cataloguing-in-Publication Data
A catalogue record for this book is available from the British Library

ISBN-13: 978-0-500-51334-7
ISBN-10: 0-500-51334-1

Printed and bound in China

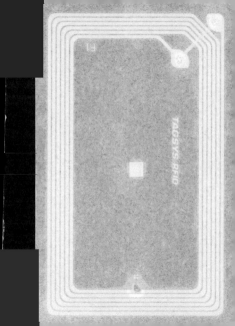